CATCH THE WIND HARNESS THE SUN

22 SUPER-CHARGED SCIENCE PROJECTS FOR KIDS

Michael J. Caduto

Storey Publishing

"This Dream is so far away,
And you feel like you will never be able to reach it. . . .
Trust me, i have had these feelings,
and i am only eleven.
It is in your grasp, it is not as far away as you think.
If you think positive and work hard
your dream will come true."

— Samantha Muscarella
Action For Nature Eco-Hero, 2009

The mission of Storey Publishing is to serve our customers by publishing practical information that encourages personal independence in harmony with the environment.

Edited by Rebekah Boyd-Owens, Sarah Guare, and Deborah Burns
Art direction by Jessica-Lynn Armstrong
Book design and text production by Vivien Sung, Studio Seed Pty Ltd.

Photography credits appear on page 223
Illustrations by © Clayton Hanmer, except for pages 67, 105, 111, 144, and 205 by Jessica-Lynn Armstrong

Indexed by Christine R. Lindemer, Boston Road Communications
Reviewed by Cynthia Grippaldi, Center for Ecological Technology (CET); Susan Reyes, Northeast Sustainable Energy Association (NESEA); Benjamin P. Luce, PhD., Lyndon State College; Marie Levesque Caduto, Vermont Agency of Natural Resources; David Bonta, USA Solar Store

© 2011 by Michael J. Caduto

Storey Publishing
210 MASS MoCA Way
North Adams, MA 01247
www.storey.com

Printed in the United States by Courier
10 9 8 7 6 5 4 3 2 1

LIBRARY OF CONGRESS CATALOGING-IN-PUBLICATION DATA

Caduto, Michael J.
Catch the wind, harness the sun / by Michael J. Caduto.
    p. cm.
Includes index.
ISBN 978-1-60342-971-9 (hardcover : alk. paper)
ISBN 978-1-60342-794-4 (pbk. : alk. paper)
1. Renewable energy sources--Juvenile literature.
2. Energy conservation--Juvenile literature. I. Title.
TJ808.2.C33 2011
333.79'4—dc22
                        2010051169

Planet Friendly Publishing
✓ Made in the United States
✓ Printed on Recycled Paper
Text: 10%   Cover: 10%
Learn more: www.greenedition.org

At Storey Publishing, we're committed to producing books in an earth-friendly manner and to helping our customers make greener choices.

These books are manufactured in the United States and are in compliance with strict environmental laws. And printing them on recycled paper helps minimize our consumption of trees, water, and fossil fuels. The text of *Catch the Wind, Harness the Sun* was printed on paper made with 10% post-consumer waste, and the cover was printed on paper made with 10% post-consumer waste. According to Environmental Defense's Paper Calculator, by using this paper instead of conventional papers, we achieved the following environmental benefits:

* Trees saved: 53

* Air emissions eliminated: 5,067 pounds

* Water saved: 24,402 gallons

* Solid waste eliminated: 1,482 pounds

CONTENTS

PART 1

HEATING UP

PART 2

CHILLING OUT

PART 3
HARNESS THE SUN

PART 4
CATCH THE WIND

PART 5

CRANK UP THE POWER

FOREWORD BY JOHN HANSON MITCHELL

f the predictions for the various disruptions associated with global climate change are accurate, sometime within the next 50 years the world as we now know it will be decidedly different. Sea levels will rise, coastal cities will flood, there will be major shifts in human population centers, plant communities will shift, and an as yet unpredictable number of species will become extinct.

The people who will be most affected by these massive alterations are now in grade school or pre-school — or have yet to be born. What that means is that this sector of the population will need to have a better understanding of the physics and biology of the forces that are causing these climatic changes and a means of better dealing with the new world they will be living in. Essentially, that is what *Catch the Wind, Harness the Sun* sets out to do. Herein you will find simple, clear, and entertaining accounts of the physics of the atmosphere, gas exchanges, wind currents, solar energy, fire, and water, as well as step-by-step directions for various experiments kids can undertake to demonstrate the actual workings of these various processes and use them to generate renewable energy.

I wish I had had a book like this when I was growing up. Science — especially physics — was profoundly boring in my time, all filled with discussions of kinetic and potential energy and electrical currents. Michael Caduto's book covers some of the same material. The difference is that it is fun to read, and more importantly, the information is essential to understanding what some scientists have termed the most profound environmental problem of our time.

John Hanson Mitchell
Editor of Sanctuary, *the Journal of the Massachusetts Audubon Society, and author of many books including* The Paradise of All These Parts: A Natural History of Boston *(Beacon Press) and* Ceremonial Time: Fifteen Thousand Years on One Square Mile *(Perseus Books)*

FOREWORD BY DAVID BONTA

When I was just a whippersnapper, a dear old man who would come to be my "guru" told me something that I never forgot. He said, "There are two kinds of people in the world — those who make the world a little better and those who make the world a little worse. Whose side are you on?"

I, of course, replied that I would like to be on the side of those who made the world better for my having been there. He said simply, "Prove it."

Ever since that day, I felt a need to at least try, in any little way, being mindful that all of us factor into the balance — no matter who we are or how young or old we are. That is why I am so happy to see Michael Caduto write this book, *Catch the Wind, Harness the Sun.*

You can participate in making the world a better place, and this is a great book to show you how to do that. It will begin to prepare you for some of the most challenging and exciting opportunities the human race has ever faced. Though this book may contain riddles and games, it takes seriously the problems we face and the need for action by you, our youngest citizens.

Big changes are coming. As we move away from regrettable and unsustainable energy choices and practices, it will mean much work. Transition could be tough. Certainly the world will change, as it must. The rewards of living in ways that sustain the Earth will bring a bright future for all.

Just as the problems of the world are all interconnected, it is a happy coincidence that the solutions are as well. When you begin, with even a small step toward a better and brighter day, then the whole world begins to be a little better off!

As we see the world develop, future energy needs will be enormous. How will we provide the secure and sustainable resources we will need? Who will be our solar technicians of tomorrow? I know it is Michael's hope, and mine, that this wonderful book will serve as your "first primer" in this all-so-important task.

It is brimming with learning and bursting out in fun! Some projects are easy, some require a bit more effort, but there are lots of hands-on things to do, and all of the activities have lots to teach you.

Hey, kids, so what kind of citizen do you want to be for planet Earth? Here's your chance to plug in to the promise of tomorrow's energy and to live in ways that keep our home planet safe, healthy, and alive. Enjoy!

David Bonta
Founder and president, USA Solar stores

PREFACE

Years ago there was a group of kids who would hang out at some local ponds in the woods near their houses in Warwick, Rhode Island. During the summer they caught frogs and turtles. When winter arrived they couldn't wait to go skating. Time passed, and the ponds became a haven for kids in that neighborhood, where most of the familiar forests, fields, and other landmarks in the town were being cut down, bulldozed, and developed.

One day, a thirteen-year-old boy from this group of kids read in the local newspaper that someone had bought the land around the ponds. That person wanted to rip up the trees, fill in the ponds, and build more than a hundred small houses called condominiums. So the boy went door to door and gathered 235 signatures to petition against the development. When he told townsfolk what was happening, a group of citizens met and formed a Neighborhood Improvement Association.

At the next meeting of the town planning board, more than a hundred people who opposed the condominiums packed the room. Town officials and the developers were dumbfounded.

This painting, "Le Châtelier's Principle Realized," was created by the author when he was 13. It contrasts dark industrial pollution with the vibrant colors and flowing energy of nature. The title is from a chemistry principle that states: When something changes and throws a system out of balance, it will react so as to form a new balance. The painting asks the question: "To which direction will the balance ultimately tip?"

The author at 13 years

...and as an adult standing in front of the wetlands he helped to save in his youth.

When the thirteen-year-old stood up and spoke to oppose the development, he was so nervous that his knees shook and he could hardly speak. He was breathing quickly and his palms were sweaty. At first he spoke very softly. But when he saw the faces of his friends and neighbors in the crowd and thought about what was going to happen to their favorite pond, his voice grew louder. He told town officials that no one wanted that development and that there were several ponds there where kids went to play. He reminded them that it was their job to advocate for the citizens of the town, not the developers. He said that if the condominiums were approved, it would show that the town didn't care what kind of place would be left for their children to live in. A few days later, the developers stopped their plans.

Nine years later, when that teen was a senior in college, he received a phone call from the Neighborhood Improvement Association. The developers were back with their proposal to build condominiums! Now twenty-one years old, he was studying wetlands ecology and land-use issues. So he again appeared before the town's planning board, this time as an expert witness, using maps and environmental protection laws to spell out restrictions on development in and around wetlands. Ultimately, some condominiums were built, but less than half the number the developer wanted. The ponds where those kids used to hang out were protected by a 200-foot-wide strip of natural land called a buffer, and are still there today.

That thirteen-year-old kid wrote this book.

Those early experiences taught me that even someone who is young can make a difference, if only that person cares enough to get organized, take action, and push for change. They showed me how we have to work hard and use our knowledge and skills. And we sometimes need to step up and fight for the things we love.

KIDS' POWER!

Catch the Wind, Harness the Sun is all about capturing and using renewable energy from the forces of nature in order to sustain the health of our planet. With these activities you can explore how to harness the sun, catch the wind, and be a Green Giant in your everyday life. *Catch the Wind, Harness the Sun* also shows how to save energy and use less of the power that comes from burning coal, oil, and natural gas — energy sources that are putting tons of carbon dioxide into the air and causing global climate change. This book is about **living in balance with the environment today in order to take care of the future.**

Catch the Wind, Harness the Sun shows how to use your personal power to make a difference. There are so many people in the world that every little bit of energy we save quickly adds up to a huge amount. If each of the 106 million households in the United States lit just one bulb with solar energy instead of with the electricity that arrives through the power grid, it would save more than enough power to light all the bulbs in 3.5 million average homes — for a whole year! So anyone who tells you "One person isn't going to make a big difference" is just plain in the dark about light.

The United States is home to 312 million people. That's less than 5 percent of the 6.8 billion people who live in the world. But even though the United States has only a small portion of Earth's peoples, **we use 25 percent of all the energy** used worldwide! On top of being such energy hogs, we get more than 85 percent of our energy from sources such as oil, natural gas, and coal. These are the *fossil fuels* that formed under pressure, and underground, from the remains of plants and animals that mostly lived even before the age of the dinosaurs.

It takes 2 million miles (3,218,688 km) of pipelines just to deliver the oil that we use in the United States. Exactly how long is that? The next time you're out on a clear night, look up at the moon and consider that our closest celestial body is really 238,856 miles (384,401 km) away. If the oil pipelines that

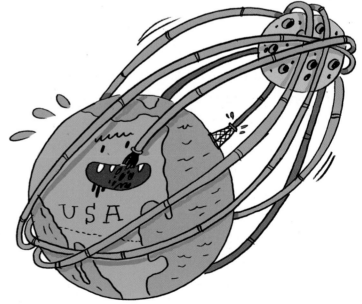

Can't get enough of this greasy stuff, glub, glub...

feed the petroleum thirst in the United States were placed end to end, they would make 4½ round trips between Earth and the moon! Our natural-gas pipelines would stretch for a bit more than a single, one-way trip.

Ours is an ever-shrinking planet thanks to energy-fed technology — a global web woven of Internet links, wireless connections, and satellite hookups. Your friend lives in China? No problem! High-speed access will bridge the gap. From YouTube, blogging, and Twitter to digital music on demand, CD-ROM, and flat-screen TV, trying to keep up with the latest innovations makes you want to, well, stream.

But there is a downside. As technology becomes increasingly cool to use, the planet heats up. Everything we do draws power from the **grid**, the web of cables that feed electricity to our homes, schools, and businesses. That power is generated mostly by burning fossil fuels, which creates more carbon dioxide and causes the global temperature to rise. Heat your home, drive to school or to a concert, and you're just one more cause of global warming. Plus you're using up sources of energy we can't replace, tapping into wells that will run dry.

Why should you care? Because it's your world — to own and to inherit. *Catch the Wind, Harness the Sun* can help you live in a way that is **sustainable** — a way that takes care of the planet so that the natural

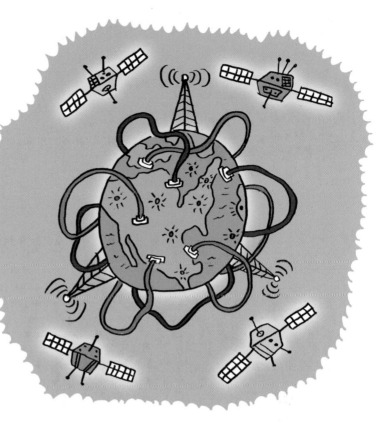

It's a World Wide Web of wired and wireless signals.

world will be able to meet the needs of your generation — and of those to come.

Who else is going to do something about it? From governments to grassroots movements, lots of people are working to find cool planetary solutions. Great numbers of kids are playing a role (check out the Green Giant profiles throughout the book), and so can you. In the long run **it's up to you, your friends, and kids you've never met** who happen to live all over this beautiful Earth. You're the ones who will help to decide what the world will become. So grab a friend and dive into this bookful of activities, from folklore to community action, from artwork to word games and riddles, from science and culture to Earth-consciousness.

HEATING UP

CHAPTER 1

ENERGY AND THE POWER OF SIMPLICITY

Simplify, Simplify, Simplify.

— Henry David Thoreau, *Walden*

What would life be like without lighting, computers, recorded music, air-conditioning, central heat, or — horror of horrors — television and video games!? Now imagine that there are no engines to drive our cars or buses; no trains, planes, or motorcycles. What difference would it make?

Consider electricity. Imagine a power plant — a sprawling factory of gigantic buildings, smokestacks, and piping where fuel is burned to create the heat that is used to generate our electricity. Now picture this: There are more than 6,000 power plants creating energy, 24 hours each day, in the United States. **Half a million miles of power lines** are needed to feed this electricity to our homes and businesses. That's enough power

lines to wrap 20 times around the equator's 24,902-mile (40,075 km) length.

In order to make this power, we have to burn the fuel that creates the fire that makes the steam that turns the turbines that generate the electrical current. Burning coal, oil, or gas makes about 86 percent of this steam. Nuclear power plants create 8 percent of the steam using powerful reactions that reach about 20,000°F (11,100°C) in order to heat water to its boiling point of 212°F (100°C). How efficient does that sound?

Isn't it time to **try something different?** Picture your own life without any of the things that use electricity. Give it a try by living through "A Dark Day of Enlightenment," which is on page 18.

FOLLOW THE JOURNEY COAL TAKES FROM THE MINE TO THE POWER LINE:

①strip-mine coal shovel, ②trucks, ③coal train cars, ④river barge, ⑤coal-fired power plant, ⑥steam boiler, ⑦electric-generating turbine, ⑧power line, ⑨house & lightbulb

GREEN GIANT

Grand 3rd Grade

Grand Prize Winner

Go Green, Go SamTrans

Kevin Huo
Audubon Elementary, Foster City

Art Takes a Bus Ride

KEVIN HUO, FOSTER CITY, CALIFORNIA

ART FOR THE EARTH

When it comes to living "Green," the palette of eleven-year-old artist Kevin Huo holds every color of the rainbow. His "canvas" ranges from the pages of a calendar to the sides of city buses in San Mateo, California. In 2008, Kevin's painting of nature in the city won first place in San Mateo's "Go Green, Art Takes a Bus Ride" competition. And one of his bright, lively illustrations was recently awarded first place in the "I Love Costa Rica's Rain Forest" art contest, which was juried by Smart Poodle Publishing.

He began as a first-grader, winning a 2006 contest hosted by San Mateo's Human Investment Project Housing Program by creating artwork that best expressed the theme "What does 'house' mean to me?" Kevin created an image called "Katrina Cottage," which showed a house like a castle, walking through floods and storm clouds — a house that could survive in a tough

situation. Kevin says that this image was meant to "remind people to care about the Earth and climate change."

Communicating with Pictures
In the fifth grade, Kevin started an art campaign called "Paintbrush" to raise people's awareness about the environment and to encourage others to work for a Green and sustainable planet.

"I used the great opportunity in the 'Go Green, Art Takes a Bus Ride' contest to get my message out to everyone so they'd understand that this Earth is getting sick. I want everyone to understand that they should ride the bus and lower their carbon footprints.

"Every day we see coastal forests burning, rapidly melting glaciers, and people throwing chemicals into the water and cutting trees. In many countries children and young people face very poor sanitation, health care, and environmental conditions. The decisions made today will have significant impact on our lives.

"We must safeguard our natural environment, with its diversity of life, its beauty, and its resources, all of which enhance the quality of life, for present and future generations," he says.

Kevin's painting of natural life in a mangrove swamp was one of only a dozen chosen from among those submitted by child artists from around the world (and the only winner from the United States) and was featured in the 2010 Children's Art Calendar, published by the Mangrove Action Project, in Port Angeles, Washington.

Because of Kevin's devotion to the environment and his many accomplishments as an eco-artist, he was among the handful of young activists chosen in 2009 to receive an International Young Eco-Hero Award from San Francisco-based Action For Nature — a nonprofit group that encourages young people to "take personal action to nurture and protect a healthy environment on which all life depends."

Strong Support and a Global Reach

Of course, no child is a "Green" island. Kevin says he's been able to take his art to such heights because he's had support from local communities and volunteer organizations, and guidance from his teachers, parents, and friends. Kevin has great appreciation for his parents, Gina Kuo and Kenneth Huo, activists and organizational leaders in many arts-and-culture, environmental, sustainable, and Green campaigns. And he speaks highly of his school principal, Mr. Rick Giannotti; his teacher, Ms. Danette Gee; and government officials and activist groups, all of whom have encouraged him.

Kevin's parents have inspired him to see the connection between taking care of people and taking care of the environment. In May 2008 there was a catastrophic earthquake of magnitude 7.9 in eastern Sichuan, China, that killed 70,000 people. That spring Kevin organized an art exchange called Paintbrush Diplomacy: fellow students at Audubon School created artwork to share with students in China. Kevin's architect father led a team of experts from California to China the following October to help with the

"THE DECISIONS MADE TODAY WILL HAVE SIGNIFICANT IMPACT ON OUR LIVES."

rebuilding efforts. Mr. Huo took the artwork created by Kevin and his classmates to China and presented it to students whose school had been destroyed by the earthquake. The project was called From Disaster to Sustainable Reconstruction — the Gansu Experience. In November, when the rebuilding team returned to California, they visited Audubon Elementary and shared stories about their fellow students in China, "half a world apart."

Clearly Kevin had a sense of his life's mission from an early age and has followed that calling faithfully. He says he loves what he does: "Through drawing and participating in the community's public arts and culture events, I helped out my parents, my teachers, my schools, my communities — and I shall continue doing it."

A DARK DAY OF ENLIGHTENMENT

How can a day without electricity enlighten you — help you see things in a new way?

PICTURE A BULB TURNING ON IN YOUR MIND. THAT LIGHT WILL HELP YOU SEE THAT IT'S POSSIBLE TO LIVE WITHOUT FOSSIL FUELS, JUST LIKE THE 1.6 BILLION PEOPLE IN THE WORLD TODAY WHO LIVE WITHOUT ELECTRICITY.

! SAFETY FIRST !

Plan this activity with parents and teachers. Work together to make a Safety First set of ground rules for handling sleepovers, candles, campfires, and any other events and activities you'll enjoy during your Dark Day of Enlightenment. *Use flames only when adults are present to supervise.*

WHAT YOU WILL NEED

Materials and supplies you'll use for this 24-hour period, such as:

* **Water**
* **Candles**
* **High-energy food that is easy to prepare and needs no refrigeration**
* **Sleeping bags**
* **Bicycle, scooter, or skateboard**
* **Games and sports equipment**
* **Books to read**
* **Notebook or journal**
* **Pen or pencil**
* **Matches**
* **Campfire-making supplies (newspaper, tinder, kindling, logs)**

DO THE DEED

Twenty-four hours — how long could that be? You can endure almost anything for only a day, right?

"No problem!" you say.

Let's see! Here's the plan: You're going to live from sunrise to sunrise without using anything that runs on electricity or relies directly on the consumption of fossil fuels. This means no lightbulbs or iPods, no battery-operated devices, no cars that burn gasoline, and no use of oil or natural gas either directly or indirectly. In order to have the most control over your situation, try Dark Day of Enlightenment on the weekend, when you don't have to go to school.

1 **Call some friends and plan activities that don't consume energy.** This means that television, computers, battery-operated games, theaters, and visits to the local mall are all out!

List and gather what you need for each activity. The better you plan, the more successful and enlightening your experience will be. Also make a list of the meals you will eat, the menu for each meal, and how you will cook or otherwise prepare them. Gather that food, and put it aside for when you need it. Be certain you have gathered everything you'll need by the start of the 24-hour period. Borrow things if you need to. If you want, plan for a practice run during part of a day.

There are many fun things to do that don't use electricity: Playing ball, biking, riding a scooter, or skateboarding.

2 **Think through every action before you take it.** Consider the sources of energy or supplies needed to do it, and make sure no electricity or fossil fuels are being consumed. For starters: Find a windup alarm clock to wake you, because the electric model sitting next to your bed is off-limits. Don't turn on the bedroom or bathroom light or get anything out of the refrigerator. Walk to where you are going, or use a scooter or bicycle, instead of riding in a car.

3 **Have fun and make an adventure out of your Dark Day of Enlightenment!** Play your favorite board games. Depending on the season, go swimming, sledding, or skating outside. Get a group together for a pickup game of baseball, basketball, soccer, or field hockey. Play Chinese checkers or double Dutch jump rope, build a fort in the woods, make fairy and goblin houses, or host a knitting circle under a cool shade tree. Plan a long hike in a natural area to pass the time and enjoy the outdoors. Recruit some friends and siblings to join you in the experience, to make it more fun and to get support so it's easier to follow through for a whole 24 hours. Get your parents involved (or not, if it's more fun by yourself). Incorporate a sleepover with friends into your Dark Day of Enlightenment. There's no end to what you can do.

4 **Keep a journal** and record all the events that occur, as well as your thoughts and feelings.

THE BIGGER PICTURE

Try to remember the things that happened during your Dark Day of Enlightenment. Use the journal that you kept to help you recall what took place and the thoughts and feelings you had during the experience. Things happened that were probably funny, challenging, frustrating, and fun — all at the same time. You could write down the experiences in the form of a story. Be creative! You could turn your story into a play to act out with friends and share with others to help them see how it's possible to survive without electricity and how comical and fun it can be when you do so!

DID YOU GO ONE WHOLE DAY, FROM SUNRISE TO SUNRISE, WITHOUT USING ELECTRICITY OR FOSSIL FUELS?

THINK ABOUT IT

- What did you enjoy the most about your Dark Day of Enlightenment? What was the most fun?
- What did you find the most challenging about this activity?
- What are some of the funny things that happened?

THINK HARDER

- Did you learn anything unexpected from the experience that really surprised you? What did you learn? How were you enlightened?
- At which times during the 24-hour period did you find the experience to be the most challenging? Why was this the case?
- If you spent your time with others, who in your group seemed to take especially well to this experience? Who seemed to struggle? What kind of character traits seemed to help with living through the Dark Day?
- Where did you spend most of your time during the 24 hours? Why was this?

NOW, REALLY THINK

- How would you do things differently if you lived in a Dark Day of Enlightenment for another 24 hours?
- Would you and your friends do this again? How about extending the experience for a two-day stretch?
- How can your Dark Day of Enlightenment experience prepare you for times when there is a power outage and the electricity goes out?
- What two or three things that you normally use could you do without? Try living without them for a few days, then a week, then a month or more.

CHAPTER 2

GLOBAL CLIMATE CHANGE

"As more and more people understand what's at stake,
They become a part of The solution."

— Al Gore

Fire is a force of nature that makes it possible to live the way we do. We need fire to create the electricity that we use every day, to power our cars and trucks, and for many other activities that we take for granted. But our use of fire has gone out of balance. Those flames are creating odorless, invisible gases that capture the Sun's heat and hold it near Earth's surface. The rising heat could change the future in ways that we've only begun to imagine.

Some of you have probably heard the term *global warming* so many times that you just don't think about it much anymore. After all, how could a rise in the average global temperature of just a few degrees be such a huge problem? What's the big deal about the few more hot summer days and milder winters that Earthlings now experience because of global warming?

Carbon is an element — one of the building blocks of life. It is within us. It is all around us. If we don't count water, carbon makes up half the weight of all plants and animals. Carbon is also found in the familiar gas *carbon dioxide*, also called CO_2.

A leaf takes in carbon dioxide
and gives off oxygen.

A MATTER OF ATOMS

Molecules are made up of atoms: tiny particles of matter that are too small to be seen. The chemical formula for carbon dioxide, CO_2, tells us that each molecule contains one atom of carbon (C) and two atoms of oxygen (O_2). Molecules may be small, but the atoms they're made of, and how they behave, are the reason the matter in the world around us looks, feels, and behaves the way it does.

CUSTOMER: What do I get if I order the carbon dioxide molecule?

WAITER: It comes with a main dish of carbon and two oxygens on the side.

A growing plant takes carbon dioxide out of the air. It also uses water and — powered by sunlight — creates the sugars it needs to grow, storing the carbon in its leaves, roots, and stems. Plants also give off oxygen. This process, called *photosynthesis*, is how the green pigment in plants, which is called *chlorophyll*, captures energy from the sun. Photosynthesis means "put together with light."

In nature, everything we do is connected to everything else, and things move in circles and cycles. When a plant dies and *decomposes*, which means it breaks down and changes back into soil, the carbon is released back into the air as carbon dioxide (CO_2). That's part of the *carbon cycle*. Normally, the amount of carbon dioxide absorbed and released by a plant during its life cycle is in balance, or about equal. This means that the

HEAT CHANGES WEATHER PATTERNS ALL AROUND THE GLOBE.

amount of carbon dioxide in the atmosphere doesn't change much because of the life and death of a plant.

When you open a soft drink and listen to the *pffftttt*, that's the familiar fizz of carbonation. But most of the carbon dioxide we create today comes out of the exhausts of our cars and trucks and rises up the chimneys of our power plants and homes. It comes from burning gasoline, oil, coal, and natural gas. There's no denying it; **we live in an industrial world of carbon-nations.**

A SWELTERING EARTH

Where did all these carbon-based fuels that we burn come from? Most coal and oil were formed from **the remains of plants** that grew before the age of the dinosaurs, back in the *Carboniferous period* more than 300 million years ago. These *fossil fuels* are made mostly of carbon. When we burn fossil fuels — coal, oil, natural gas, and things like gasoline that are made from oil — carbon from these ancient, long-buried deposits is ultimately released back into the air. This happens much faster than the plants growing today

Burning fossil fuels creates smog, acid rain, and other kinds of air pollution, including the carbon dioxide that is contributing to global climate change.

❶ oil deposit

❷ oil well

❸ oil-fired power plant to electrify our homes

❹ air pollution

can absorb it. So carbon dioxide is building up in the atmosphere — it has increased by 30 percent since fossil fuels began to stoke the furnaces of industry back in 1850.

So what? Picture a perfect day at the beach. The Sun is shining, waves are breaking on the sand, and you lie there taking in some rays. Now imagine what it would feel like if someone came along and used a plastic sheet to create a small greenhouse over you and your beach blanket. The plastic would allow *solar* (the Sun's) energy, called *radiation*, to enter, but it would also trap the heat that reflects back from the sand. In a short time, you would begin to swelter as the temperature climbed past 110°F (43°C). You wouldn't be able to stand it, it would be so hot! Moisture would start to build up on the inside of the plastic. Your thirst would become unbearable.

That small greenhouse is the extra carbon in the atmosphere, and you are Earth experiencing the **greenhouse effect.** Now imagine the same thing happening to the entire Earth, our lovely home planet, and you have a bad case of global warming. (Methane and nitrous oxide are two other gases people add to the atmosphere that can trap the Sun's heat.)

Gases in the atmosphere act like a greenhouse wrapped around our Earth.

Often, global warming is called **global climate change.** That's because the greenhouse effect alters more than just Earth's temperature. Heat changes weather patterns all around the globe. As a result, some environments, like the northeastern United States, are becoming wetter. Other regions, especially Africa, are drying out.

CARBON-NATION SIMULATION

A real greenhouse is full of growing, green plants. But there's nothing Green about the greenhouse effect.

CARBON-NATION SIMULATION IS A SIMPLE EXPERIMENT TO HELP YOU SEE HOW CARBON DIOXIDE CAUSES GLOBAL WARMING.

WHAT YOU WILL NEED

* Scissors

* Two 1-liter or 2-liter plastic beverage bottles

* Two inexpensive weather thermometers that will fit completely inside the plastic beverage bottles when the tops are cut off

* A sheet of clear plastic wrap big enough to completely cover the top of one cut-off beverage container

* Tape or rubber band, to seal plastic over the mini greenhouse

* Notebook and pencil, to write down temperatures

! SAFETY FIRST !

Use scissors carefully to avoid cuts. Once you've trimmed the plastic bottle, the top edge can be sharp and should be handled with caution. Most thermometers have a fragile glass tube filled with liquid, and so need to be treated gently to avoid breaking the glass.

DO THE DEED

Here's a simple way to simulate how the greenhouse effect works.

1

3

Use scissors to cut off the narrow part of the top from both plastic bottles, and remove the labels. This will create two widemouthed plastic containers.

2 Place a weather thermometer inside each beverage container so the bulb is at the bottom.

Now stretch a sheet of clear plastic wrap over the top of one bottle. Make sure the edges are sealed well with the tape or a rubber band. *The plastic represents the invisible extra carbon dioxide, methane, and nitrous oxide released into the atmosphere by human activities.*

4 Place both bottles in direct sunlight.

5 Watch and wait until the temperature stops climbing on both thermometers so that you get a true reading of the temperature inside the containers. Read the thermometers and write down the temperatures of both bottles in a notebook.

Think of the temperature in the open bottle — without plastic over it — as the surface temperature of Earth without excess greenhouse gases in the atmosphere. Think of the temperature in the bottle covered with plastic as the surface temperature of Earth with excess, heat-trapping greenhouse gases in the atmosphere.

6

Compare and record the temperatures in both bottles over the course of an entire day — from when you rise until bedtime. Keep track of the times when the Sun is up and when it is below the horizon.

What does this data tell you about how the plastic affects the temperature in the covered bottle when the Sun is out and when it is not?

THE BIGGER PICTURE

On a small scale, this experiment shows how global warming can happen. These questions will help you sharpen your powers of observation to figure out what happened in the two bottles.

THINK ABOUT IT

⊘ Which is higher: the temperature in the greenhouse bottle or the temperature in the uncovered bottle?

⊘ Why do you think one temperature is higher than the other?

THINK HARDER

⊘ What caused this result? Can you explain how it happened?

⊘ What does this demonstrate about how greenhouse gases can affect the temperature on Earth?

NOW, REALLY THINK

⊘ Try this activity both ways: using two 1-liter bottles and two 2-liter bottles. Was the temperature difference between the two 1-liter bottles larger or smaller than the temperature difference between the two 2-liter bottles? Why?

CHAPTER 3

A NOT-SO-GREEN HOUSE

Q. What size carbon shoe do you wear?
A. One big enough to fill your carbon footprint.

What's a **carbon footprint?** We all use a certain amount of energy and materials to keep us alive and to live the way we choose. Bigger houses and cars use up more energy than smaller ones. So does always buying the latest electronic gadgets, because it takes supplies — like metal and plastic and lots of energy — to make and ship them to the stores. The more energy used, the more carbon dioxide and other greenhouse gases are created.

Your *carbon footprint* is the amount of carbon dioxide and other "greenhouse" gases that are created when supplying the energy and materials that keep you alive and support your way of life.

We in the United States are Carbon Bigfoots. Numbering about 312 million people, we make up just 5 percent of the world's population, **yet we produce 24 percent (almost one quarter) of all the carbon emissions on the planet!** About 11 tons (10 metric tons) of carbon dioxide enters the atmosphere each year just to supply the energy used by a typical household in the United States.

How much is 11 tons of carbon dioxide? Think of it this way: The tiny Smart Car weighs about 1 ton, or 2,000 pounds, with the driver in it. So that means your family releases around 11 Smart Cars' worth of carbon dioxide into the air every year while using your TV, washer and dryer, lights, computers, and other electric appliances.

That's a lot of carbon per family! And if you add the carbon produced from using gasoline, diesel, and other fuels for transportation, your carbon footprint grows even larger.

CARBON BIGFOOTS STOMP ON OTHER COUNTRIES

More than 1 billion people live in the 100 or so countries that are most seriously threatened by changes brought on by global warming. These countries are mainly in Africa, Asia, and South America. But many of these people are poor and live simple lives, so they only create about 3 percent of all the carbon emissions that are turning our planet into a giant greenhouse.

For example, in Malawi, a country in southeastern Africa, the average household earns about $250 per year, and 40 percent of this money is earned by growing crops. Many of Malawi's people are very poor. Weather changes that are a result of global warming are causing both floods and droughts, even though Malawians create almost none of the world's carbon dioxide emissions. Growing seasons are short so it's hard for the people of Malawi to grow enough food to eat. Diseases are spreading and proper medicines to care for the sick are scarce. So people living in Malawi, and in other countries that have the smallest carbon footprints, are being affected in very serious ways by climate changes caused mostly by people who live in Carbon Bigfoot countries.

In our power-based economy, **almost everything we do consumes energy,** even if it doesn't involve plugging in to an electrical outlet. Baseball and soccer are healthy outdoor sports, but most people hop in the car and drive to the playing fields. Drinking water from plastic bottles? The plastic is made from petroleum, and when the bottle is thrown out **it will be in a landfill for thousands of years.** And the grapes you munch on at halftime could have been shipped from other continents, often in refrigerated trucks and cargo ships that eat up lots of fuel.

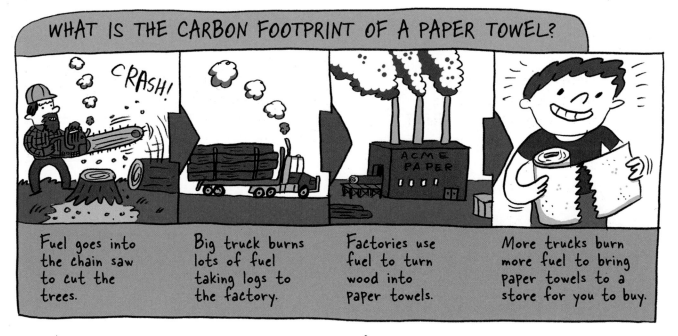

WHAT IS THE CARBON FOOTPRINT OF A PAPER TOWEL?

CRASH!

ACME PAPER

Fuel goes into the chain saw to cut the trees.

Big truck burns lots of fuel taking logs to the factory.

Factories use fuel to turn wood into paper towels.

More trucks burn more fuel to bring paper towels to a store for you to buy.

➡ Paper towels are convenient, but a lot of energy is used to make them. Try using a dish towel or cloth napkin instead of a paper towel.

ARE YOU A BIGFOOT?

Want to figure your carbon footprint? The easiest and most accurate way is to do it online. Take the following steps:

1 Type "Carbon Calculator" into Google or whatever Web search engine you use on your computer. Ask a parent or teacher for help if you're not sure how to do this.

2 Click on a website that has a carbon calculator and follow the instructions.

3 You may be asked whether you want a Quick, Simple, or Detailed calculation of your carbon footprint. When choosing, keep in mind that the detailed calculation will be the most accurate but requires some numbers from your parents' electric and heating bills.

4 Once you've answered the questions, the calculator will then estimate the carbon footprint, which means it will tell you the number of tons of carbon dioxide your entire household releases into the atmosphere each year.

The United States has only 5 percent of the world's population, but it produces a lot of carbon emissions for its size.

5 If you want to know your personal carbon footprint, divide this household number by the number of people who live in your home.

The death of a tree cuts both ways. Once a tree is felled (cut down), it stops growing and can no longer absorb carbon dioxide from the atmosphere. And when the dead wood is burned or decays, the carbon stored within is released into the air as CO_2.

CUTTING DOWN TREES, BUILDING UP POLLUTION

In fact, most of our activities are connected to other activities that require energy for them to happen. This usually means burning oil, gasoline, coal, or natural gas, all of which emit carbon dioxide into the atmosphere. And there are other unhappy results of our busy lifestyle. For example, every tree that is cut down for wood or to be made into paper releases CO_2 into the atmosphere. This CO_2 contains the carbon that was stored in its trunk and leaves. (Remember what happens during photosynthesis?) But that's not all. Because that cut tree is no longer growing, it won't be storing any more carbon over time.

Altogether, 33 million acres (13,354,626 hectares) of trees are cut around the world every year — patches of forest that together add up to be as big as the state of Alabama.

The trees cut in tropical rain forests alone add 1,650,000,000 tons (1,496,854,821 metric tons) of carbon to the atmosphere annually, which is about the weight of **165 million school buses!** Cutting trees makes up one-fifth of the entire greenhouse gases created every year.

There are other gases besides CO_2 that cause Earth's temperature to rise, such as water vapor, methane, nitrous oxide, ozone, and *CFCs* (gases used in refrigerators and air conditioners). Methane comes from bacteria living in marshes, in bogs, and on the ocean floor. It also spews out of the mouths of volcanoes and wafts up from manure and cow burps. And a ton of methane traps 20 times more heat in the atmosphere than does a ton of carbon dioxide. So you can see why the planet is heating up!

WHAT GIVES WITH GREENHOUSE GASES?

Many gases that enter our atmosphere can act in the same way that the glass on a greenhouse does, trapping the Sun's heat.

Here are the most important greenhouse gases and their human sources:

CARBON DIOXIDE is created when we burn fossil fuels. The greatest amount comes from burning coal (especially to make electricity), followed by oil and natural gas. Carbon dioxide makes up about 80 percent of the greenhouse gases that are created by people.

METHANE comes from producing oil and natural gas and from the gas found in coal mines. Raising livestock and growing rice create a lot of methane, which also gases off when trash and manure decompose. And, yes, cows do burp and fart methane. Fortunately, most of it comes out of the front end.

OZONE can be confusing. There is too much of it in the lowest layer of air (the *troposphere*), which traps the Sun's heat. At ground level, nitrogen oxides and carbon-containing gases from car exhausts, factories, and burning forests react with sunlight to create ozone.

But in some places there is not enough ozone in the next-highest layer of air (the *stratosphere*). That's the so-called hole in the ozone layer. This hole allows more of the sun's harmful radiation to reach Earth's surface.

NITROUS OXIDE comes from burning fossil fuels in factories, cars, trucks, and other vehicles. It is also given off by sewage treatment plants and when nitrogen fertilizers are made. (Dentists sometimes use nitrous oxide [laughing gas] so that their patients don't feel any pain, but there's no evidence that this causes global warming.)

CFCS (chlorofluorocarbons) are found in refrigerators, air conditioners, and powerful liquids used for cleaning. They were once used in spray cans, but that use was banned. In the atmosphere, CFCs can last more than 100 years. CFCs not only add to global warming. They also add to the destruction of the upper layers of the ozone.

WATER VAPOR is the most common greenhouse gas, but its atmospheric level adjusts naturally because it can precipitate as rain and snow. However, as the atmosphere heats up, more water evaporates from lakes, rivers, and oceans, which also adds to global warming. So... the warmer it gets, the warmer it tends to become. Get it?

OTANA JAKPOR, RIVERSIDE, CALIFORNIA

CLEARING THE AIR ON OZONE

Some people were born to change the world, but they fulfill that destiny only because they discover an injustice and possess both the willpower and the courage to do something about it. Otana Jakpor is one of those people.

"I was twelve years old when I started my ninth-grade science fair project," says Otana. "I chose to investigate 'Indoor Air Pollution: The Pulmonary Effects of Ozone-Generating Air Purifiers and Other Ozone-Generating Household Devices.'"

That seems like a huge topic for a twelve-year-old, but Otana's report was only the beginning of a remarkable journey. In May 2006 Otana read a *Consumer Reports* article that said some indoor, ionizing air cleaners give off high levels of ozone, an unhealthy greenhouse gas. Although air purifiers are advertised to improve breathing, some air purifiers emit harmful ozone.

"Some people who are dear to me use air purifiers," said Otana, "so I wanted to determine whether these air purifiers are helpful or harmful for breathing."

Otana's mother has severe asthma that requires sensitive monitoring equipment to measure how well her lungs are functioning.

"I knew that I could use these devices to measure pulmonary function and conduct a study testing friends and family in my own home to determine the truth about ozone-generating air purifiers," says Otana. "My mother has been my inspiration because of her daily battle with severe asthma."

Principles of Science Lead to Discovery

"First, I prepared a careful research project following the scientific method. I did background reading, then came up with a hypothesis. I borrowed pulmonary testing equipment from my mother and an ozone sensor from Eco Sensors, Inc. After several weeks of 'science experimentation parties' — where I invited friends to come to my house to watch movies and, after informed consent, be guinea pigs — I had my results.

"My findings were extremely alarming. The ozone-generating air purifiers and food purifier, a device that uses ozone to kill bacteria in food, tested reduced pulmonary function, especially among asthmatics. One asthmatic even had a drop of 29 percent in an important measure of pulmonary function (FEV1/FVC), and an acute asthma attack. The ozone-generating room air purifier, personal air purifier, and food purifier, respectively, produced staggering concentrations of ozone — about 15 times, 9 times, and 3 times higher than a Stage 3 Smog Alert. These findings were too important for me to simply leave as a successful science fair project."

Otana soon discovered that her project had two important elements of success: (1) a strong basis in facts and (2) good timing. Otana's results came just when the California legislature had passed a bill that directed the California Air Resources Board (CARB) to create a law to limit ozone emissions from indoor air purifiers. Otana shared her data with the members of CARB as they were writing up their new regulations and again at a hearing in September 2007, when the new law took effect.

"AIR POLLUTION ...IS ONE OF THE GRAVEST ENVIRONMENTAL THREATS IN NORTH AMERICA."

Representatives from the businesses that make and sell air purifiers, and their lawyers, attended these hearings. "A common line," says Otana, "was, 'You have no direct evidence that these machines are harmful.'"

In fact, Otana's research findings clearly showed that ozone purifiers were harmful. After witnessing all the testimony, CARB voted to adopt a regulation to limit ozone emissions from air purifiers to less than 50 parts per billion (ppb). Otana's scientific evidence supported the passage of these laws.

Real Change for a Better Tomorrow

Proudly, Otana points out that "California is the first state in the nation to regulate ozone generators. Most people spend over 90 percent of their time indoors, and the California Air Resources Board estimates that indoor air pollutant levels are often 25 to 62 percent greater than outdoor levels."

Otana's remarkable research and testimony was rewarded in a big way when, in April 2008, she received the President's Environmental Youth Award from President George W. Bush at a ceremony in the Rose Garden of the White House.

"This wonderful opportunity opened the door to more chances for public policy advocacy," Otana declared. "I continue to testify at Environmental Protection Agency [EPA] hearings on air quality and am now a volunteer spokesperson for the American Lung Association. Also, I have met with both the previous and the current U.S. EPA administrators and urged them to set tighter outdoor ozone standards."

Otana has published her study in the *American Journal of Respiratory and Critical Care Medicine* and is now researching air pollution created by candles.

"Air pollution is not just a personal issue of concern for my family; it is one of the gravest environmental threats in North America. According to the Earth Policy Institute, 70,000 lives are lost to air pollution in the U.S. annually — a number equal to deaths from breast and prostate cancer combined. In Southern California alone, fine-particle pollution is estimated to cause about 5,400 premature deaths per year, which is comparable to deaths from traffic accidents and secondhand smoke."

JOIN THE GREEN SCENE

Otana Jakpor's website (see Resources) provides information about air pollution and ideas for getting involved: becoming informed, educating others, writing to government officials, testifying at public hearings, and joining the American Lung Association's Healthy Air Walks.

BLUE-BURNING MARSH BUBBLES

To see the blue-burning marsh bubbles aglow, you'll first need to collect methane from the muddy muck of a pond or marsh.

DEEP IN THE MUCK, **MICROSCOPIC BACTERIA BREAK THINGS DOWN** ANAEROBICALLY — WITHOUT THE USE OF OXYGEN — AND CREATE METHANE GAS. YOU CAN LIGHT THIS GAS ON FIRE TO CREATE HEAT.

WHAT YOU WILL NEED

* Pair of old, sturdy, high-topped sneakers or rubber boots for mucking around in a marsh or the marshy end of a pond

* Wide-mouth, quart-size Mason or Ball jar with screw-on lid (the kind of glass jar used for canning food that has a lid with a separate ring and top works best); *do not use a container larger than a quart jar (about 1 L)*

* Wide-mouth funnel with an opening of at least 6 inches (15 cm) across

* Towels, for drying off

* Box of long wooden matches

! SAFETY FIRST !

Have a parent, teacher, or other trusted adult help you with this project. The activity requires supervision because it involves mucking around in a pond and lighting a flame outdoors.

The second part of the project must be done in a very safe place where there is no fire hazard (especially in fire-prone western states or under dry conditions), such as a protected outdoor fireplace in a campground or a paved parking lot. *If you live in a dry area or where there is an elevated fire hazard, do not do part II.*

If you're not sure if the area you live in is safe or want to find a place to try lighting the fabulous blue flame, ask a parent or call your local fire department.

DO THE DEED

If you always thought energy was hard to find, this experience is sure to pop your bubble.

PART I: BUBBLES IN THE MUCK

1 In the late afternoon on a warm day, take a walk with other kids and your adult helper down to a pond or marsh. This should be a shallow body of water with a mucky bottom and a bank that's clear of trash and debris, especially broken glass.

2 Put on your heavy sneakers or boots and pick up the quart jar and the funnel.

3 Place the cap to the jar in a pocket where you can easily reach it as you muck around in the marsh.

THE METHANE MAKERS

As bacteria in the muck consume plant and animal matter, they also create methane, ammonia, and hydrogen sulfide, which smells like rotten eggs.

4

Wade into the edge of the pond or marsh, and be careful to stay in the shallows. This type of habitat has a way of becoming very deep in just a few steps!

Be sure to keep your jar underwater for Steps 5-9

5

6

7

Submerge the jar, open-end up, and allow it to fill up with water.

Keep the jar completely underwater, and turn it over so that the opening faces down. You will see the bottom of the jar facing you beneath the surface of the water.

Insert the narrow end of the funnel into the mouth of the underwater jar so that the wide part of the funnel faces the bottom of the marsh.

Now carefully begin to muck around, pushing into the mud with your feet while holding the mouth of the funnel over where you are stepping. Your steps will release gas bubbles that rise into the funnel and jar and take the place of the water inside. **Keep the jar absolutely level while you hold it underwater;** don't tip it from side to side or the bubbles will escape.

8 Keep mucking around and catching bubbles until almost all the water in the jar has been displaced (pushed out) by marsh gas.

9 **Keep the jar facing down underwater as you remove the funnel.** With the jar still facing down, place the cap over the opening and screw it on tight.

Now you can take the jar out of the marsh. If the seal on the lid is snug, you can keep the jar for a short while and don't have to light it (part II) immediately. It's fine if there's a little water in the bottom of the jar.

PART II: LIGHT ON!

Wait until dusk and find a place outdoors that is fairly dark but away from any low-hanging branches, leaves, or tall grasses that could catch fire. Bring your adult helper, the jar, and the matches to that spot. This should be a protected campground fireplace, sandlot, pavement (far away from any cars), or other fire-safe area.

Ask the adult to help with the steps for lighting your marsh-gas torch. Before you light the marsh gas, **be sure everyone's hands and faces are off to the side and away from the top of the jar** because a flame will flare up about 10 inches (25 cm) high from the mouth of the jar.

1 Place the jar on the ground. Have an adult light a long match and hold the flame close to the mouth of the jar while keeping her or his hand off to the side and away from the top of the jar.

2

Quickly take the cap off the jar and move it off to the side while your adult helper holds the lighted match at the edge of the jar's opening.

3

As soon as the cap is removed and the gas is lit, move all hands away from the bottle and put out the match. Methane will continue to rise up from the jar, creating a pale blue marsh-gas torch that will burn for 10 to 20 seconds, depending on the size of the opening and how much gas is in the jar.

RAP ALONG WITH MUCK MAN

(Make up your own tune.)

Marsh-Gas Rap

Who knows a feeling that can beat
the feel of mud beneath our feet?
It slips and slides between the toes
that walk among the cattail rows.
The bubbles that come floating up
live in the gushing, oozing glup.
And if they meet a lighted match,
beware the blue, hot marsh-gas flash.

THE BIGGER PICTURE

From marshes and ponds to trash heaps and farms, methane is all around us, even though you can't see it or smell it. Human activity creates about two-thirds of all the methane that enters the atmosphere every year. Of all the methane that comes from natural sources, two-thirds is given off daily by marshes and other kinds of wetlands. Here are some questions and activities to help you discover methane and how it can be used for energy.

THINK ABOUT IT

- Why does the methane rise out of the jar full of marsh gas when it is uncapped?

- What did you notice about the flame?

- If you had a lot of methane to burn, what could you use it for?

- Cows create a huge amount of methane, so in what job do you think people have an excellent opportunity to burn methane for heat and to create electricity?

THINK HARDER

Landfills, also called garbage dumps, generate huge amounts of methane as our buried trash decomposes anaerobically (in the absence of oxygen).

- Because landfills create methane, how could we reduce the amount of methane being produced?

- How could methane be captured so that we can burn it as a fuel?

- Considering the health of the environment, do you think methane would make a better fuel than coal, oil, and natural gas? Why, or why not?

- Could you harvest a little methane for fuel? How would you do it? Sketch your invention in the box on the next page.

NOW, REALLY THINK

How much methane does the marsh you visited create each day? To find out, first you'll need to figure out the size of the marsh. An **acre** is a square that measures about 208.7 feet on each side, or that totals 43,560 square feet. An acre of marsh or wetland, which is really a shallow pond that is no more than about 6.5 feet (2 m) deep, gives off 90 cubic feet of methane every day. That's enough methane to fill the back of a large SUV. (A **hectare** is a square that measures 100 meters on each side, or 10,000 square meters. One hectare of marsh produces 6.3 cubic meters of methane each day.)

1 Start by measuring the two distances along the shore of the marsh where it is longest and widest.

2 Multiply the length and width to get the number of square feet (or square meters).

3 Divide this number by 43,560 square feet (or 10,000 sq m if calculating hectares) to estimate the size of the marsh in acres. (Since the marsh is round and won't fill the corners of a rectangle of that length and width, the actual size of the marsh will be a bit smaller.)

4 Now multiply this number of acres by 90 cubic feet (or 6.3 cubic m if using hectares) to get a rough number of the cubic feet (or cubic meters) of marsh gas given off by that marsh each day.

METHANE HARVESTER

Sketch your invention here.

How much marsh gas is produced in your neighborhood each day? Get a *topographic (topo) map* of the area around your home or school. This is a map that shows elevation — how high the hills and mountains are and how low the water bodies are compared to sea level. Find the ponds and marshes in your area and, using the map's key, estimate the number of acres or hectares they cover. Multiply the number of acres by 90 cubic feet (or the number of hectares by 6.3 cubic meters) to estimate the volume of marsh gas produced in your neighborhood each day.

How much carbon dioxide would it take to trap the same amount of heat that methane traps? Methane traps 20 times more heat from the Sun than carbon dioxide does. Multiply the volume of methane being generated in your neighborhood by 20 to find out how much carbon dioxide it would take to trap the same amount of the Sun's heat.

____ cubic feet/meters of methane x 20 =
____ cubic feet/meters of carbon dioxide

WHAT ARE SOME OTHER NATURAL SOURCES OF METHANE?

Scientists and teachers at PolarTREC (Teachers and Researchers Exploring and Collaborating) are studying how global climate change is causing the Arctic environment to warm and how this may cause carbon dioxide and methane to be released into the atmosphere. Visit the following website to learn about their work and to contact the PolarTREC scientists directly to ask questions:

www.polartrec.com/arctic-tundra-dynamics-08

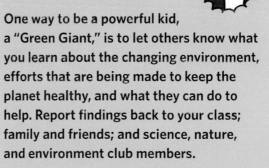

JOIN THE GREEN SCENE

One way to be a powerful kid, a "Green Giant," is to let others know what you learn about the changing environment, efforts that are being made to keep the planet healthy, and what they can do to help. Report findings back to your class; family and friends; and science, nature, and environment club members.

PART 2

CHILLING OUT

CHAPTER 4

WHERE HAS ALL THE POWER GONE?

"Come, Watson, come! The game is afoot."

— Sherlock Holmes in *The Adventures of the Abbey Grange,* by Sir Arthur Conan Doyle

Is energy mysteriously disappearing from your house? Are your parents spending a lot of money on energy bills? If so, an Energy Thief may be afoot.

You may not be able to tell if your family is losing energy — and money — just by looking at the electric and heating bills. You have to do some real detective work to find out where precious energy is slipping away unnoticed.

JOIN THE GREEN SCENE

In addition to the energy-wasting ways that appear on page 47, the next activity will show you ways in which energy is being stolen.

WATT'S A WATT?

When empowered kids talk about electricity, they use words for their measurements that you'll want to know about.

Watt is the standard unit used to measure electrical power. One **kilowatt** equals 1,000 watts. One **megawatt** is 1 million watts. Power plants generate so much electrical power that their output is usually measured in megawatts.

Kilowatt-hours measure the amount of electrical energy you consume (check your electrical bill). The power consumed, multiplied by the length of time, calculates the energy used. For example: a 60-**watt** lightbulb × 100 **hours** of use = 6,000 **watt-hours** ÷ 1,000 = 6 **kilowatt-hours**. (1,000 watt-hours = 1 kilowatt-hour).

SIGNS OF ENERGY THEFT

Here are some clues that an Energy Thief is present. We'll discuss later (page 59) how to bring these thieves to justice by saving energy.

WASHING AND DRYING

- Washing machine running with a small load
- Washing machine using hot water
- No clothesline in the yard, out the window, or on the porch or balcony
- Clothes dryer being used on a sunny day

APPLIANCES

- Refrigerator with a leaky rubber seal around the edge of the door
- Refrigerator with dusty, dirty grille
- Use of unnecessary appliances
- Electrical devices with an "instant on" switch using power even when turned off

- Appliances running with no one using them, such as the television, computer, stereo, and fan

LIGHT

- Lightbulbs that are too bright for family's needs
- Incandescent lightbulbs
- Light switches that mysteriously get turned on every time someone turns them off
- Lights turned on in a bright room during the day

HEATING AND COOLING

- Air conditioners set too low (below 75°F [24°C] when people are home and below 80°F [27°C] when they are away)
- Heating thermostats set too high (above 68°F [20°C] when people are awake, above 60°F [16°C] when asleep, or above 50°F [10°C] when away)
- Unwrapped hot-water pipes in the basement
- Water-heater temperature set too high (over 120°F [49°C])
- Doors and windows with a draft of air seeping through the bottom or around the frame
- Someone browsing the refrigerator for food while holding the door open

OHMS

Ohm is the unit that measures how resistant a substance is to conducting (or passing along) electricity. The symbol for ohm is Ω. For example, aluminum is a good conductor but doesn't conduct electricity as well as copper, so aluminum wiring carries a higher rating for ohms.

SHERLOCK OHMS & DOCTOR WATT-SON

Thieves are stealing energy from your home. As the resident detective, you have been put on the case to uncover the clues that reveal how the energy is disappearing.

LEARN WHAT YOU CAN DO TO STOP THE THEFT OF ENERGY IN YOUR HOME AND REDUCE YOUR ENERGY USE IN THE FUTURE.

! SAFETY FIRST !

A good detective does not disturb the scene of a crime — she looks but does not touch. As you play the sleuth, stay away from live wires, electrical outlets, hot pipes, running motors, and other potential hazards.

WHAT YOU WILL NEED

* Pencil

* Clipboard or cardboard and paper clip, for backing

* Copy of the pages torn from the notebook of detectives Sherlock Ohms and Doctor Watt-son (see next page)

DO THE DEED

1 Place a copy of Ohms & Watt-son's Detective Notebook on a clipboard or clip it to a piece of cardboard for support as you write. Or if this book is yours, open it to pages 50–53.

2 Move from room to room in your house, and search for clues to how energy is disappearing. Go slowly and observe closely. Imagine how Sherlock Holmes would search for clues to an energy thief.

3 Every time you find a place where an energy thief is striking and valuable energy is being wasted, mark the cause of the energy loss in the left-hand column of your Detective Notebook. (Some clues are found in the Signs of Energy Theft list on page 47.)

WATT-SON

OHMS

THE BIGGER PICTURE

Can you think of ways to foil the energy thieves? Now that you have completed your sweep through the house and recorded energy loss in your Detective Notebook, it's time to solve each case of stolen power and take action!

1 **Examine your theft list. Do you notice any patterns in your list of energy culprits? Do you see the same kinds of things (and people) in each room sucking up energy unnecessarily? Who and what are the biggest wasters?**

2 **In the right-hand column of your detective sheet, write down actions you might take to "return" the "stolen" energy to a room by reducing energy use in the future.**

3 **Can't figure out how to keep more energy loss from occurring? Well, you're in luck. The section called "How to Shrink Your Carbon Footprint" in the next chapter describes ways that you and your family can stop the energy thieves. Match each clue in your Detective Notebook with an action on pages 59–63.**

4 **Create an original version of a detective notebook, one that records the things that people in your house are already doing to save energy.**

OHMS & WATT-SON'S DETECTIVE NOTEBOOK

These pages taken from the notebook of famous detectives Ohms and Watt-son will help you search for clues that energy is disappearing in each room in your home. Once you have completed a room-by-room examination and inventory of the theft, read How to Shrink Your Carbon Footprint, on pages 59–63, for ways to take action to thwart the energy thief.

OHMS

Energy Theft

Action to Take to Stop the Theft

Write down actions you might take to "return" the "stolen" energy.

Kitchen

Coffeemaker plugged in but not on   (Unplug it to stop phantom power drain)

Living Room

Dining Room

Bedroom

🔍 _____ (_____.)

🔍 _____ (_____.)

🔍 _____ (_____.)

Bedroom

🔍 _____ (_____.)

🔍 _____ (_____.)

🔍 _____ (_____.)

Bedroom

🔍 _____ (_____.)

🔍 _____ (_____.)

🔍 _____ (_____.)

Den or Recreation Room

🔍 _____ (_____.)

🔍 _____ (_____.)

🔍 _____ (_____.)

🔍 _____ (_____.)

Office

🔍 Computer monitor on, not in use (_____.)

🔍 _____ (_____.)

🔍 _____ (_____.)

🔍 _____ (_____.)

Energy Theft	Action to Take to Stop the Theft

Entryways or Halls

_____ (_____)

_____ (_____)

_____ (_____)

_____ (_____)

Bathrooms

_____ (_____)

_____ (_____)

_____ (_____)

_____ (_____)

_____ (_____)

Laundry or Workroom

_____ (_____)

_____ (_____)

_____ (_____)

_____ (_____)

Basement

_____ (_____)

_____ (_____)

_____ (_____)

_____ (_____)

Attic

🔍 _____ (_____)

🔍 _____ (_____)

🔍 _____ (_____)

🔍 _____ (_____)

Barn/Garage

🔍 _____ (_____)

🔍 _____ (_____)

🔍 _____ (_____)

🔍 _____ (_____)

Outside/Surrounding House

🔍 _____ (_____)

🔍 _____ (_____)

Other Room

🔍 _____ (_____)

🔍 _____ (_____)

🔍 _____ (_____)

🔍 _____ (_____)

Other Room

🔍 _____ (_____)

🔍 _____ (_____)

🔍 _____ (_____)

🔍 _____ (_____)

WATT-SON

CHAPTER 5

POPPING THE CARBON BUBBLE

"Just as the problem is the sum of what each one of us is doing, so is the solution."

— Anthony D. Barnosky, author of *Heatstroke: Nature in an Age of Global Warming*

Wilma Rudolph, the famous Olympic gold medalist who was known as the fastest woman in the world, once said, "The triumph can't be had without the struggle." It is easy, when faced with a big problem, to become discouraged and think that whatever you can do is too small to make a positive change. In fact, your actions play an important role in the bigger story about all of the people who are taking care of our world.

We can all do our part to reduce our carbon footprint (see page 59) and help Earth chill. Everything we do that saves energy cuts down on the amount of carbon dioxide that is created when generating that energy. You could be a **Light-Switch Watcher**, making sure that lights are turned off when everyone has left a room. How about becoming a **Monster** **Degree-Monger** who keeps the thermostat in a comfortable but energy-efficient zone (see Heating and Cooling, on page 60).

If we all reduce our carbon footprint by a matter of degrees, it quickly adds up to taking a big step!

SMALL CHANGES ADD UP

Did you know that if you unscrew one incandescent bulb and replace it with a compact fluorescent lightbulb *(CFL)* you are taking a small but important step toward reducing the destructive greenhouse effect? And when we lower our use of electricity, we cut down on the release of greenhouse gases from the power plants that create electricity. The electricity saved by changing that single old-fashioned bulb to an energy-saving CFL can, during the life of that bulb, reduce the amount of carbon dioxide that would have been created to make that electricity by 1,000 pounds (454 kg).

You can make other changes around the house that are good for the environment. For example, hanging clothes outdoors (a Green practice that could be called drying clothes "on-line") and washing your clothes in cold water use much less energy. These practices produce only **one-tenth of the carbon dioxide** of a routine using a hot-water wash cycle and a traditional clothes dryer. Let's do the math to understand why.

There are 106 million households in the United States. Each load of wash done

The average car burns about 1,860 calories of energy to move a passenger one mile. Taking a train or public bus uses about half this much energy. For each mile you ride in a car, you use the same amount of energy as biking for 50 miles (80 km). You can pedal a bike more than 800 miles (1,288 kilometers) using the same amount of energy contained in one gallon of gasoline!

with a conventional wash cycle and clothes dryer uses enough energy to generate up to 7 pounds (3.2 kg) of carbon dioxide. So how much carbon dioxide is generated every time all of the households in the country wash and dry one load of clothes? See the box below.

If every household washed one load of clothes each week with cold water, then air-dried those clothes on a clothesline, this would reduce the amount of carbon dioxide emissions produced for those loads, nationwide, by 90 percent. That means 668 million pounds (303 million kg) less carbon dioxide would enter the atmosphere. Now that's letting a lot of gas out of the carbon bubble!

Here is the math:

106 million households × **7 pounds (3.2 kg)** of carbon dioxide per load = **742 million pounds*** (337 million kg) of carbon dioxide per one U.S. load of laundry.

* The volume of 1 pound of carbon dioxide is 8.2 cubic feet (in a cool room at sea level), about the capacity of a super-size clothes dryer!

PRINCESS FIREFLY'S LOVERS
(A traditional tale from Japan)

Why do we waste energy? Science offers the knowledge and know-how for us to better understand the world. But what do we do with the facts and figures? How do we use them to understand our personal habits? How do we change our ways to live sustainably? Wisdom shows us how to use knowledge in order to make good decisions that will take care of Earth and other people.

Here is a traditional folktale from Japan. As you enter the world of this story, try looking beneath the surface to understand what it says about the attraction of fire and other things that can bring us happiness, unless we get too close to them or have too much of them.

On a moonlit night during the seventh month, a breeze rocked the crimson petals of a lotus floating on the marsh. Cradled in this flower sat Hotaru, Princess of the Fireflies. Her golden light was a blazing star on a sky of dark water.

Up she flew among the lotus petals, past the wildflowers and out over the rice fields. Hotaru's light worked its spell. Hundreds of suitors followed, struck by her beauty.

At last Princess Hotaru again came to rest on the petals of her lotus bloom.

Hundreds of suitors followed, struck by Hotaru's beauty.

Scarlet Dragonfly flew bravely toward the flame.

"Please," cried each of the suitors who landed near Hotaru, "take me for your husband."

"One alone shall win my heart," she replied.

"What must we do?" they asked.

"You must bring me a gift of fire," she declared. "Show me that you love me more than life itself."

"This I will gladly do," said Golden Beetle.

"I will not return without your gift of fire," declared Hawkmoth.

"Neither of you can fly as swiftly as can I," boasted Scarlet Dragonfly.

The three suitors flew off into the night. Scarlet Dragonfly saw a flickering flame where a young girl sat at her desk and read a love letter by candlelight. Her tears fell onto the parchment. Dragonfly flew bravely toward the flame to snatch a bit of fire for Hotaru. Instantly, his wings were singed.

"Oh, how sad!" cried the girl, "Why did you fly into the fire?" Scarlet Dragonfly lay lifeless upon the desk.

Golden Beetle buzzed to a house where a woman sat mending clothes by the fireplace. Golden Beetle whirred past the woman's left ear, causing her to jump. There was a crackling and a flash in the fireplace, then a puff of smoke drifted up with the sparks.

"What could that have been?" asked the woman. She rose from her chair and found the toasted beetle upon the hot coals.

In time, Hawkmoth fluttered toward a house where a student was reading by the light of an oil lamp. Hawkmoth flew close to the flame, but the student brushed him away. Then Hawkmoth plunged into the candlelight and burned his wings. He fell into the thick lamp oil, struggled, and drowned.

Continued on the next page

There was a crackling and a flash in the fireplace as Golden Beetle landed there.

Meanwhile, Hotaru waited safely within the petals of her lotus bloom. As she gazed at the stars, a golden light streaked across the sky. "It must be a falling star!" she thought. The light came closer until Hi-Maro, Prince of the Fireflies, perched upon a petal at the edge of Princess Hotaru's lotus. Hi-Maro unfolded his wings to reveal the brilliant flame of life within. Hotaru leapt with joy at the sight.

"I have come to ask you to be my wife," said Prince Hi-Maro. He flew up over the marsh and his golden, dancing starlight captured Hotaru's heart. The prince and princess were wed later that night. Generations of fireflies have lived amid the lotus petals ever since.

To this day, during the time of the seventh moon, Princess Hotaru's suitors fly through the darkness on their quest for a gift of fire. One after another, they throw themselves into the flames: tall candles in Buddhist temples, lamps in the courtyards of shrines, kitchen lanterns, and sparks streaking from chimney tops. Each morning, people find the places of night fire littered with bodies. "Look," they say, "many lovers tried to win the heart of Princess Firefly last night."

Hawkmoth plunged into the lamplight.

"I have come to ask you to be my wife," said Prince Hi-Maro.

The story of Princess Firefly could be a symbol of our modern lives. The firefly Princess Hotaru is like all those things we want to fulfill our dreams of happiness. But first, we must have fire. Energy-consuming toys, gadgets, tools, and appliances are our Princess Hotarus — those things we could not have without the gift of fire that creates our energy supply.

So, like Golden Beetle, Hawkmoth, and Scarlet Dragonfly, we spend our time seeking the flames. In our hunger for more and more energy to power a way of life that we find so attractive, we throw ourselves into the fire. We often make unwise decisions by wasting energy and using sources of energy that harm Earth and each other.

Is it any wonder that Princess Hotaru chooses Prince Hi-Maro, who is also a firefly? About 90 percent of a firefly's energy is used to make light, unlike incandescent lightbulbs, which waste 90 percent of the energy they use by producing heat. The most energy-efficient lights that we can now obtain, which are called light-emitting diodes, or *LEDs*, convert nearly 80 percent of the energy they use to pure light! Incandescent bulbs and other devices that use a lot of energy are like the fire-seeking insects in the story. But energy-efficient lights are our Princess Hotarus and Prince Hi-Maros.

HOW TO SHRINK YOUR CARBON FOOTPRINT

You already know some of the ways that we waste energy (see page 47). Included in the following sections are many simple things that you and your family can do to save energy and help to reduce global warming. There are lots of great opportunities here for getting your parents involved.

"BRIGHT" LIGHTS

- **Better bulbs.** Replace the incandescent lightbulbs in your room with compact fluorescent lightbulbs or LED lightbulbs and encourage your parents to do the same with other lights in your home.

- **Smart use.** Use lights only when you need them — and turn them off when you leave the room.

- **The joy of soy.** Use candles made from soy wax rather than candles made from paraffin wax. Paraffin is made from petroleum oil. Soy wax candles, which are made from soybean oil, create less soot as they burn, and they don't smell like paraffin or create harmful hydrocarbon emissions. Choose candles that don't have wicks made out of lead, which is released when a candle is burned.

- **Let the sun shine in.** Open a curtain or window shade to let in sunlight, instead of turning on a light.

- **Not too bright.** Install lightbulbs that are only as bright (wattage) as you really need.

WATER — HOT AND COLD

⊘ **Tolerate tepid.** Use as little hot water as possible when washing up.

⊘ **Don't let it run.** Turn off the water in the sink while you brush your teeth and wash up.

⊘ **Shower light.** Take short showers (10 minutes or less) and install a water-saving showerhead.

⊘ **Wrap it.** If the hot-water pipes in your basement are bare and not insulated, wrap them with pipe insulation. Wrap your water heater in an energy-saving, insulating cover.

⊘ **Wash when dirty.** Use your towel and clothes until they need to be washed, rather than throwing them into the laundry basket after every shower or bath. Wait until there's a full load before washing.

⊘ **Choose cold.** Wash clothes in cold water.

⊘ **Not so hot.** Ask an adult to set the temperature of your water heater to 120°F (49°C), which is hot enough.

⊘ **Save with the Sun.** If your family can afford it, encourage your parents to install a solar water-heating system and/or a system that creates electricity from the Sun (a photovoltaic system). Solar water heating brings big savings.

HEATING AND COOLING

⊘ **Warm is cool, but hot is not.** During the cold season, turn the thermostat down to 68°F (20°C) when people are awake and down to 60°F (16°C) when they are asleep.

⊘ **Be cool, but not too cool.** During the summer, cool your house only as much as needed and use fans when possible. Turn up the temperature to 75°F (24°C) when people are home and to 80°F (27°C) when they are away.

⊘ **Capture cool.** Let cool air in at night and seal it in during the day. Draw shades that are in the sun.

GETTING AROUND GREEN

⊘ **Punch your ticket to the Green-Line Express.** Instead of taking a car on your next trip around town, walk, ride a bicycle, or take a bus or train.

⊘ **Don't drive alone.** If you must take a car, try to carpool with other families and kids.

⊘ **Mileage matters.** Ask your parents to drive a car that gets good gas mileage.

SHOP SMART

- **Bulk is better.** Buy food in bulk from bulk bins, then clean and reuse the plastic or paper bags and other containers. It takes less energy to clean and reuse containers than it does to make new containers out of recycled materials.

- **Buy recyclables.** Buy drinks and food that come in recyclable bottles and cans rather than throw-away containers.

- **Bag the paper.** Use cloth shopping and school-lunch bags rather than bags made from paper and plastic.

- **Don't dump; sort it out.** Recycle as much of your waste as possible instead of throwing it away. It takes a much larger amount of energy to make new containers than it does to make them out of recycled materials.

- **Rags are riches.** Use old or tattered cloths for rags to clean messes off surfaces and dust the furniture instead of buying paper towels or dusters.

- **Go with Green garments.** When it comes to caring for Earth, even hand-me-downs are looking up. Pass down your old clothes to a younger sibling, cousin, or friend. Visit the consignment shop instead of the shopping mall. Go retro with your fashion statement; what's old is new!

SAVING PAPER

- **Cut your junk mail off at the pass.** Take your name off mailing lists that send out unwanted, wasteful junk mail. Call the order department and ask to have your name taken off its mailing list and removed from the information it shares with other companies. Here are a couple of websites that will enable you to accomplish this:

  www.ecocycle.org/junkmail

  http://mailstopper.tonic.com

- **Reuse.** Use recycled paper products for everything from writing pads to toilet paper and paper towels.

- **Cloth-kins.** Use cloth napkins that can be washed after a few uses rather than paper napkins.

- **Write thing to do.** Use the blank sides of scrap paper for notes before recycling them.

EASE ELECTRICITY USE

- ⊘ **Press "off."** Turn off your computer if you're not going to use it again for another hour or more. Turn off TVs and radios when no one is watching or listening.

- ⊘ **Sock-et to surge strips.** Plug your computer, television, radio, and other electronic devices into surge strips, then turn off the surge strips each night before going to bed. This eliminates the "phantom" energy use that these devices consume in order to power the features like "instant-on" switches, which use energy even when a device is turned off.

- ⊘ **Even better: Back away!** Get off the computer and go outside and play with your friends. Everything from baseball to field hockey and soccer to swimming is a recreational form of play that saves electricity.

- ⊘ **Clock out.** Take a time out from digital clocks. Turn off the digital clock feature on electrical appliances where they're not needed.

- ⊘ **Choose food first.** Decide what you want from the refrigerator before opening the door to reduce how much cold air escapes. Then take several foods out of the refrigerator at once to prevent opening the door several times. Never stand with the door open while browsing for food. Leave grazing to the cows in the fields and the deer in the woods.

APPLIED APPLIANCE SCIENCE

- ⊘ **Ditch the dryer.** Use nature's "air dryer" rather than your electric hair dryer. Not only does this save electricity, but it's also healthier if your hair is not constantly exposed to the hair dryer's high, dry heat.

- ⊘ **Fresh air's fine.** Dry clothes by hanging them on a line. If you must use a clothes dryer, keep the filter clean to save another 5 percent of the energy used.

- ⊘ **Junk the clunkers.** Encourage your parents to replace old appliances with those that are energy efficient. Remind them to bring the old appliances to a neighborhood recycling center so some parts can be reused and the rest recycled.

- ⊘ **Fix fridge leaks.** If the rubber gasket on your refrigerator door is leaking cold air, ask your parents to buy and help you install a new rubber gasket that fits your particular refrigerator. (Test the seal on your refrigerator door by putting a dollar bill between the door and the refrigerator, closing the door, and then trying to pull out the bill. If the seal works well, the bill won't come out easily.)

PLANT A GREEN FUTURE

When it comes to taking action to save energy, small is beautiful, and every action adds up over time, especially when lots of people chip in. It's also good to think large and long term. Here are some ways that you can go Green with a capital *G*:

- **Plant trees and shrubs.** Green plants take in carbon dioxide as they grow and store the carbon in their tissues and in the soil. This reduces the amount of carbon dioxide in the atmosphere. Trees also create habitat for wildlife.

- **Be shady.** Make your house as well insulated as possible to save on the energy used for heat and air-conditioning. Plant a deciduous shade tree on the southwest or southeast side of your house to cool things off in the summertime.

- **Eat less meat.** Meat from cows (hamburgers, steak), pigs (ham, pork sausage), and other livestock has a much higher carbon footprint than a similar amount of food calories from fruit, grains (cereal, bread), vegetables, and other plant foods. The animal industry creates about one-fifth of all greenhouse gases.

Mmm... veggie-licious!

- **Go local.** When you do eat meat, choose grass-fed meat that is grown locally and organically. This kind of meat has a smaller carbon footprint than meat grown on megafarms because it takes less energy to feed animals grass instead of grain and less energy when shipping, processing, and selling the meat locally. Burning less energy creates less carbon dioxide.

ORGANIZE THYSELF

- **Write the power.** Send a letter to your power company encouraging it to make as much electricity as possible from renewable sources, such as wind, solar, tidal, and geothermal power. Ask if your parents have the option to buy renewable power from the company rather than power that is made from nuclear energy or by burning coal, oil, or natural gas.

- **Ask lawmakers to be cool.** Write to your representatives in local, state, and federal governments to urge them to present and support laws that will help solve the problem of global warming.

- **Get a group.** Join organizations that are working to reduce global warming, such as the Climate Action Network (CAN) International and the Environmental Defense Fund. The contact information for these groups and others can be found in the Resources section at the back of this book.

SAMANTHA MUSCARELLA, LONG ISLAND, NEW YORK

CLEANING PARKS, SAVING THE WORLD

Samantha Muscarella took her first step as a Green Giant even before she entered first grade, on a day when she and her mom went out to play in the park.

"One day, when I was five, I was in the park and noticed it was not clean," she recalls, "so I invited my preschool and kindergarten friends to come help me clean it up. My mom and I went to the store and we bought T-shirts. On the backs of the shirts we wrote **Save the World** and drew hands coming together to symbolize teamwork, and on the front we drew a world. It was a cold day when we went to the park. We all had on our winter coats, with our T-shirts over our coats. We used brooms to sweep up the parking lot. We picked up cans, cigarette butts, and other garbage and put them into garbage bags. That Clean the Park project, in Elmont, New York, was my first project."

Green Activism Is Contagious

Samantha has since responded whenever she felt that something needed to be done to save Earth: "I initiated the recycling program at my elementary school with the help of the assistant principal. I contacted the superintendent's office, sanitation department, and the school principal. We obtained recycling bins and got volunteers to bring the bins to the appropriate spots. My assistant principal arranged the schedule with the volunteers I recruited. I was also able to get a donation of reusable bags to give teachers to promote less garbage and waste."

One day Samantha realized that to save the world she'd have to spread the word, so she and a friend started a school newspaper. Samantha wrote articles about environmental issues.

Like other Green Giants, Samantha can think of many people who inspired her and things she learned about the environment that spurred her into action. "I was always concerned about saving the animals, trees, and Earth since I was little," she says. "In school we would get a weekly reader that presented articles about saving the animals, what's happening to the ozone layer, and trees. . . . This made me interested in joining an environmental club." After she joined the Sierra Club and the National Arbor Day Foundation, Samantha donated trees to her town and her school and then helped to plant them. "The trees can help with global warming," she says.

"I have received help from many people. My family is extremely supportive in all that I do. Friends helped to plant the trees, clean the park, and do recycling and the school newspaper.

"I WAS ALWAYS CONCERNED ABOUT SAVING THE ANIMALS, TREES, AND EARTH SINCE I WAS LITTLE."

The town of Oyster Bay helped with getting materials for the Clean the Park project I started in the third grade. We all worked together. Without everyone's help, these projects would not have succeeded," she says.

Like other Green Giants, Samantha believes that "obstacles" are not roadblocks; they are things "that need to be overcome." This optimism shines through in the saying that she created for Clean the Parks: **"Flowers Bloom and Our Parks Are Groomed."**

In 2009 Samantha's many good works received local and international recognition. In addition to being recognized as one of the 2009 "Kids of Distinction" by the town of Oyster Bay, New York, she was honored with an International Young Eco-Hero Award by the environmental group Action For Nature.

Now in middle school, Samantha realizes how important her first successful experience was: "If I hadn't done that first Clean the Park, all of my other projects wouldn't have happened. My first project was an inspiration to continue to make the world a better place."

Speaking from Experience

It's not surprising that someone who began to Save the World when she was five years old has already developed a philosophy about life at age eleven.

Samantha Muscarella has also raised puppies for Canine Companions for Independence, an organization that provides trained assistance dogs and support for people with disabilities.

"I know you have probably heard people tell you to always pursue your dreams throughout your life," she says. "Those people are right. I also know that sometimes you could have this great idea and then you start to think about how much work and time it is going to take, and then you start to doubt. But you know this idea is really great and could possibly put a big impact on the world.

"So if you have any ideas that are out of this world, my advice is to go for it!"

TREE-MENDOUSLY COOL

Ever notice how tree-mendously cool a tree can be? On the next warm, sunny day, try relaxing under a spreading oak, pine, or maple tree to escape from the heat of the Sun.

DO YOU THINK IT IS COOLER IN THE SHADE ON THE GROUND OR UP IN THE BRANCHES? THIS ACTIVITY WILL HELP YOU FIND OUT, AND PROVIDE SOME CLUES AS TO **WHY TREES HELP US ALL COOL DOWN.**

WHAT YOU WILL NEED

✱ **Ball of string**

✱ **Pair of scissors**

✱ **Four inexpensive household wall thermometers (or one thermometer and a lot of time)**

✱ **Pad of paper and a pencil or pen**

DO THE DEED

1 Find a full-grown tree that casts deep shade and that has at least one branch low enough to the ground that you can reach it.

2 Cut two pieces of string: The first piece must be long enough to wrap around the tree's trunk at the height of your shoulders, plus an additional 12 inches (30 cm) for tying a knot. The second piece has to reach up and over a lower branch of the tree so you can hang a thermometer among the leaves.

3 Thread each piece of string through the upper hole on a thermometer, and fasten it with a knot.

4 Wrap the first piece of string around the tree so the thermometer is hanging as high as your shoulders, then tie it off.

5 Throw the end of the string attached to the other thermometer over the low branch on a tree. Pull the thermometer up among the leaves and then tie the string around a branch to hold it in place, as high as you can make it reach.

6 Place the third thermometer on the ground, in the shade at the base of the tree.

7 Step out into the sunshine and put the fourth thermometer on the ground in direct sunlight.

8 Wait about 15 minutes, or until the readings on all four thermometers have adjusted to the temperature of the air around them and have stopped changing.

9 Write on your pad the date, the time of day, and the temperatures of all four thermometers:

Ⓐ Shoulder-high on the tree trunk: ____°

Ⓑ Up in the leaves: ____°

Ⓒ In shade on the ground at the base of the tree: ____°

Ⓓ In direct sunlight on the ground: ____°

Why do birds, squirrels, and tree frogs make their homes in trees? Do they know something that we don't? Temperature in and around a certain place can be affected by amounts of sunlight and shade, how much sunlight is reflected, the strength of the wind, how moist the air is, and whether something faces north or south. Besides providing shade, the water evaporating from leaf surfaces cools the air in a tree's crown. (To feel the same cooling effect, try moistening the back of your hand and then blowing on it.) Trees also cast their shade on buildings, so air conditioners don't have to work as hard.

Through the activity in their leaves, trees also take carbon dioxide out of the air and store it in stems, trunks, and roots. A full-grown maple tree sprouts about 200,000 leaves, which take 48 pounds (22 kg) of carbon dioxide out of the atmosphere every year. One acre of trees absorbs about the same amount of carbon dioxide in a year as an average car would create while driving around the world. So even though thermometer readings can vary from one side of a tree to another, trees can also affect the temperature of the globe by absorbing carbon dioxide and slowing down global warming. When it comes to trees, it's all a matter of degrees.

Grab a pair of binoculars and search the trees in your neighborhood for signs of animals, like this American Robin that stands guard over its nest.

THINK ABOUT IT

- ◎ What did you learn from your measurements of the temperature in the different places in and around the tree? Where is the temperature warmest? Coldest? Why do you think that is so?

- ◎ Visit different kinds of trees, including broad-leaved trees and evergreens, and take the four temperatures described in this activity. Which kinds of trees seem to keep the air coolest compared to the surrounding temperature in the sunlight?

- ◎ Move the thermometers to different locations to measure the temperature differences. For example, is it warmer in the shade where the tree bark faces the sun, compared to the other side of the tree in the shade? Why or why not?

THINK HARDER

- ◎ Take the temperatures of a tree at the edge of a body of water (a pond, a lake, a river, or the ocean) and of a tree growing next to a paved area. Which temperature readings were cooler and which hotter? Why do you think this is so?

NOW, REALLY THINK

- ◎ Try taking temperatures of trees during the winter months. What do the winter temperatures tell you about trees that you may not have known had you only done the experiment in the summer?

- ◎ What are three ways that trees help to keep you, and the planet, cool?

JOIN THE GREEN SCENE

One billion pounds of carbon dioxide would be taken out of the atmosphere if every family in the United States planted a single tree. If you want to keep the planet cool, plant a tree.

CHAPTER 6

GLOBAL HEART-WARMING

You must be the change you wish to see in the world.

— Mahatma Gandhi

JOIN THE MARCH TO KEEP THE SOUTH POLE POLAR!

SOUTH POLE

Penguins are cool. They live on the ice in Antarctica. If they could talk to us, they'd make a real flap about global warming because their ice is melting rapidly.

Thousands of species of animals and plants are endangered by global climate change. The ways of life of hundreds of millions of people around the world are also threatened. **This means their lives are threatened, too.**

The most vulnerable environments are found:

- **Where melting ice and snow threaten to change the local habitat**

- **Where the higher sea levels created by water released from this melting are covering landmasses close to sea level**

- **Where changes in weather patterns are causing severe drought**

So global warming poses the greatest threat to:

- **Polar environments and mountain glaciers**

- **Islands**

- **Large river deltas**

- **Deserts (especially in Africa)**

VULNERABLE RIVER AND RIVERSIDE RESIDENTS

Consider the Ganges River. It starts with a trickle of water that flows from an ice cave that is 10,300 feet (3,140 m) high in the southern range of the Himalayan mountains. As it flows nearly 1,600 miles (2,575 km) toward the Bay of Bengal in the Indian Ocean, it drains a vast area of land that is up to 400 miles (644 km) wide in places. When it nears the bay, it is joined by the Brahmaputra River to form a 200-mile- (322 km) long delta — the greatest on Earth. This delta, which is mostly swampland, straddles India and Bangladesh.

This gigantic river system is home to the **susu**, or *Ganges River dolphin*, one of only four species of freshwater dolphins in the world. The susu has big flippers; a long, thin nose; and a stout body. Almost blind, these dolphins often swim sideways and search for food by feeling the bottom with a flipper. Because they are affected by water pollution and

The endangered susu, or Ganges River dolphin.

become tangled in fishing nets, their numbers have dropped. There are fewer than 2,000 living today.

As global warming causes more glaciers to melt, sea levels keep rising. Saltwater is creeping farther up the mouth of the river and into the aquatic home of the susu. Since the susu can't survive in saltwater, its habitat is shrinking.

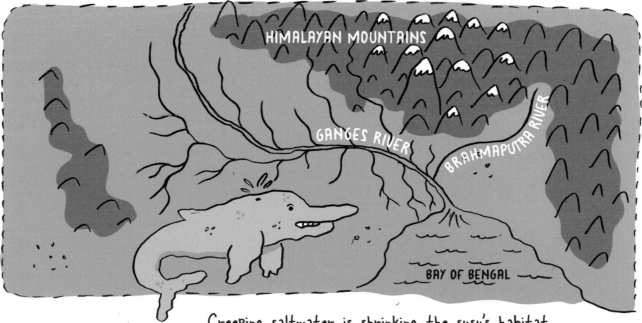

Creeping saltwater is shrinking the susu's habitat.

BANGLADESH

The homes of 8 million Bangladeshis may flood in the coming years.

The sea is also flooding the delta lowlands, where many people of Bangladesh live and grow their food. This causes hunger, homelessness, and loss of jobs. In fact, some 8 million Bangladeshis may need to move in the coming decades because of the rising waters.

So the people of Bangladesh have been forced to take actions that have resulted in a lot of hard work and changed their lives dramatically. They're raising riverbanks to prevent flooding and building shelters where people can go to be safe during storms. But if the glaciers keep melting, and the waters continue to rise, the Ganges River will one day wash over these barriers and cause more floods.

ISLAND INHABITANTS IN JEOPARDY

Also in the Indian Ocean, lying southwest of the tip of India, is the island nation of Maldives. All told, nearly 1,200 luscious tropical islands of coral and sand rest on top of ancient volcanoes and cover about as much land as Washington, D.C. Nearly 300,000 people live in Maldives. Hundreds of exotic birds and other animals are seen there, such as the Maldivian little heron, pygmy killer whale, great hammerhead shark, and five kinds of sea turtles. But the highest point in Maldives is only 8 feet (2.4 m) above the surface of the sea. If ocean levels keep rising because of global warming, Maldives could be completely underwater within a century.

Global warming also affects people who rely on catching fish to supply protein in their diet. Many of the countries affected the most by global warming get from one-third to one-half of their protein from fish each day. As oceans and freshwater lakes become warmer, they produce less of the nutrients that feed the fish that live there. **Fish populations will begin to drop.** People living in South American countries like Peru and Colombia would then catch fewer of the sardines and anchovies that they need to eat. Other countries that could be especially affected are Somalia, Myanmar, Kiribati, and the Solomon Islands. Even landlocked countries like Uganda could catch fewer freshwater fish.

MALDIVES
If the Indian Ocean rises just 8 feet (2.4 m), Maldives will be underwater.

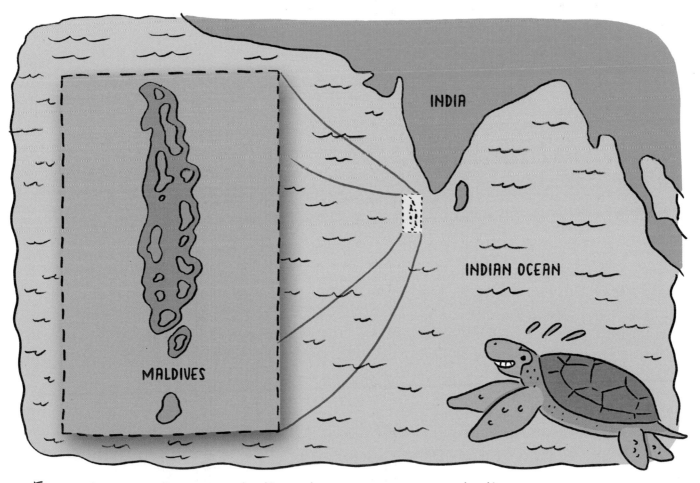

Flooded beaches will mean no turtle nests, so no eggs or sea turtles.

GREEN GIANT

PLEASE STOP KILLING ME

DON'T LITTER

CAMERON OLIVER, ABU DHABI, UNITED ARAB EMIRATES

CAMPAIGNING FOR CAMELS

Even arid countries in the Middle East are being affected by global climate change. Deserts are becoming hotter and dryer while rising sea levels are gradually flooding coastal areas.

Citizens of the United Arab Emirates (UAE) consume almost as much energy per person as those in the United States, and like us, their country is being affected by global warming. But leaders in the UAE are now taking giant steps to cut their country's carbon footprint. For example, the planned city of Masdar will be a carbon-neutral metropolis where cars will not be allowed. UAE is also working to cut down on its use of water, much of which comes from the desalination (removing salt) of water in the Persian Gulf — a process that consumes a lot of energy.

The UAE is a land mostly of deserts, sand dunes, bush country, and rocky crags, where little vegetation grows. Until the early 1960s, agriculture, herding, fishing, and pearl harvesting were the major sources of income for many families. But since that time, earnings from the country's rich reserves of oil and natural gas have brought wealth and the kind of environmental problems that come with it.

Preserving a Desert Icon

One young environmental activist from this arid land is Cameron Oliver. Although he's concerned about global warming and his country's carbon footprint, Cameron is working hard to make sure that footprints of a different kind will continue to appear in the desert sands.

Originally from South Africa, Cameron arrived in the United Arab Emirates with his family in 2007. He soon discovered that one-third of all camel deaths were caused by trash that these magnificent animals were eating. "As South Africans," says Cameron, "we are very aware of nature and wildlife, so it comes naturally for me to protect and be concerned with the environment." After reading an article in the *Gulf News* about the plight of camels in the UAE, Cameron, then eleven years old, decided to increase people's awareness of the issue as the focus of a school project.

He learned that camels and other animals mistakenly eat litter because they think it's food. Litter that is dropped by people when they are hiking, camping, riding horses, and even driving in their cars blows around in the environment. Plastics, such as bags, bottles, ropes, cutlery, cups, and can holders (for instance, six-pack rings), are a major culprit. From the ocean to the desert sands, litter is everywhere. Animals eat the litter, and it becomes stuck in their digestive systems, making it hard for them to digest and absorb their food. If they don't choke on the litter,

"IF I DON'T TRY AND MAKE A DIFFERENCE, MY CHILDREN WILL ONLY READ ABOUT CAMELS IN BOOKS."

PLEASE **STOP** KILLING ME
DON'T **LITTER**

www.cameronscamelcampaign.com

many animals slowly starve as their stomach and intestines become clogged with litter, and they experience a slow, painful death.

Spreading the Message

After researching the issue, and with help from his mother, Cameron created a logo and set up a website showing the plight of camels. He then went to the media and received lots of press coverage, from radio and Reuters television to magazines and newspapers like the *Gulf News* and *The National.* Cameron was also invited as the guest of the producer and director to the screening of *Plastic Planet* at the Middle East Film Festival. In addition to working on the camel-awareness campaign, Cameron says he is now "speaking at school assemblies, campaigning in shopping malls by handing out my T-shirts and bumper stickers, and getting my bumper sticker onto the taxis."

Because the UAE is a hot, dry country that values water and survival under harsh conditions and is working on sustainability, it is understandable that leaders are impressed with Cameron's efforts. In fact, Cameron's Camel Campaign won the 2008 Abu Dhabi Award from His Highness Sheikh Mohammed bin Zayed Al Nahyan, Crown Prince of Abu Dhabi (the capital of the UAE), from among 43,000 nominations. This, says Cameron, brought "great recognition

and awareness to stop the killing." Cameron's work received even wider acclaim when he received the 2009 International Young Eco-Hero Award from Action For Nature.

Cameron's passion comes through when he says, "Everyone can make a difference, no matter how small it is. As my dad says, 'Every river starts with one small drop of water.' I am not giving up, even though the camels are still dying every day. I will continue to campaign until our camels stop dying, as I want my children to see live camels. If I don't try and make a difference, my children will only read about camels in books."

HELPING COUNTRIES ON THE HOT SEAT

The first step toward helping countries on the hot seat is connecting with the people and the natural world in which they live.

THIS ACTIVITY WILL HELP YOU GET TO KNOW THE PEOPLE AND ANIMALS WHO ARE LIVING IN THE AREAS **MOST AFFECTED BY CLIMATE CHANGE.** BY CONNECTING WITH THE PEOPLE, AND THE NATURAL WORLD IN WHICH THEY LIVE, YOU JUST MAY FEEL COMPELLED TO HELP THEM AND OUR PLANET IN ANY WAY YOU CAN.

WHAT YOU WILL NEED

* List of countries (provided on page 78)
* A map of the world
* Bulletin board
* Online computer access
* Printer and paper

* Tacks or tape
* String or yarn
* Blank paper
* Marker

DO THE DEED

1 Choose one of the countries from the list of those that are being hardest hit by the impacts of global warming.

2 Find that country and mark it on a map of the world. Post that map on a bulletin board or wall to remind yourself of where that country is located.

3 Go online and research the plants, animals, and people from that country. Print some photos. (A list of animals on each continent that are threatened and endangered by global warming is on page 219.)

4 Post these photos on a school bulletin board or on the wall of your room, near the map. With a tack or tape, hang a piece of yarn between the country and the photos of the plants, animals, and people who live there.

5 Post a sheet of blank paper that you will use to record your activities. Each time you do something to help solve the problem of global warming, such as the actions listed in "How to Shrink Your Carbon Footprint (see pages 59–63)," use the marker to record what you've done.

6 Look at the photos you've posted, and remind yourself that — if enough people do their part — we can help people, plants, and animals in distant lands to survive and live there happily for generations to come.

GLOBAL WARMING HOT SPOTS
(COUNTRIES Arranged by continent)

1 Africa
(the entire continent)

Algeria
Angola
Benin
Botswana
Burkina Faso
Burundi
Cameroon
Cape Verde
Central African Republic
Chad
Comoros
Democratic Republic of Congo
Djibouti
Egypt
Equatorial Guinea
Eritrea
Ethiopia
Gabon
Gambia
Ghana
Guinea
Guinea-Bissau
Ivory Coast
Kenya
Lesotho
Liberia
Libya
Madagascar
Malawi
Mali
Mauritania
Mauritius
Mozambique
Namibia
Niger
Nigeria
Republic of Congo
Rwanda
São Tomé and Principe
Senegal
Seychelles
Sierra Leone
Somalia

South Africa
Sudan
Swaziland
Tanzania
Togo
Tunisia
Uganda
Zambia
Zanzibar
Zimbabwe

2 Antarctica

The entire continent

3 Asia

Afghanistan
Bahrain
Bangladesh
Bhutan
Cambodia
Laos
Maldives
Myanmar
Nepal
Pakistan
Singapore
Timor Leste
Yemen

4 Australia and Oceania

Cook Islands
Fiji
Kiribati
Marshall Islands
Micronesia
Nauru
Niue
Palau
Papua New Guinea
Samoa

Solomon Islands
Tokelau
Tonga
Tuvalu
Vanuatu

5 Europe

Cyprus
Malta
Netherlands
Russia (Arctic region)

6 North America

Antigua and Barbuda
Aruba
Bahamas
Barbados
Belize
Canada (Arctic region)
Cuba
Dominica
Dominican Republic
Greenland
Grenada
Haiti
Jamaica
Netherlands Antilles
Saint Kitts and Nevis
Saint Lucia
Saint Vincent and the Grenadines
Trinidad and Tobago
United States (Alaska/Artic region)
US Virgin Islands

7 South America

Colombia
Ecuador (Galapagos Islands)
Guyana
Peru
Suriname

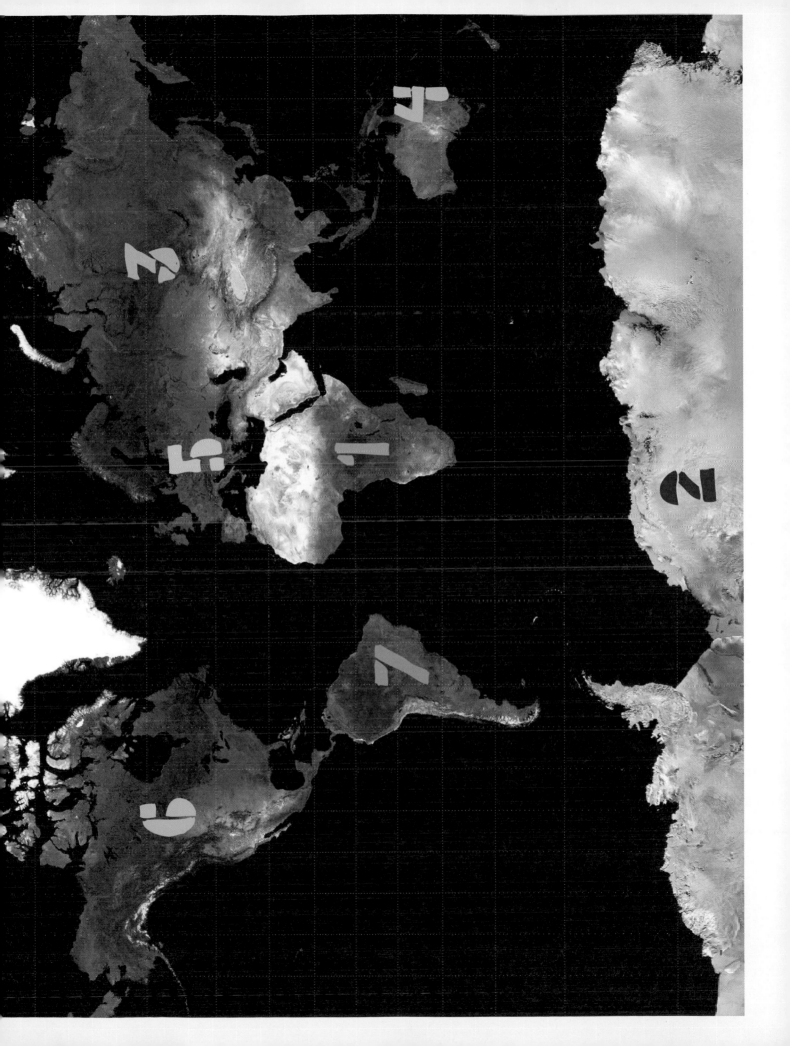

PART 3

HARNESS THE SUN

CHAPTER 7

STAR POWER

"Arise, fair sun, and kill the envious moon."

— William Shakespeare, *Romeo and Juliet*

The Sun is our home star. This great ball of heat and light, this round mass of fire, was called Sol in ancient Rome and Helios in Greece. According to a legend from the Muskogee (Creek) peoples of the southeastern United States, the Sun was carried aloft on top of a vulture's head, inside a silken bag woven by Grandmother Spider. On bright, sunny days, when the light is just right, you can still see gossamer rays of Grandmother Spider's bag shining down.

Even though the Sun is more than 93 million miles (150 million km) away, we can feel its heat and light as though it were close by. Just how far away is the Sun? If there was a road that led from Earth to the Sun, your family could climb into the car and drive there. But get out your iPods and earbuds, then download a ton of songs, because a ride to the Sun is going to take awhile.

Let's say that, on the road to the Sun, the driver brought the car up to 70 miles per

Sit back and enjoy the ride to the Sun — only 152 years to go!

The full Earth

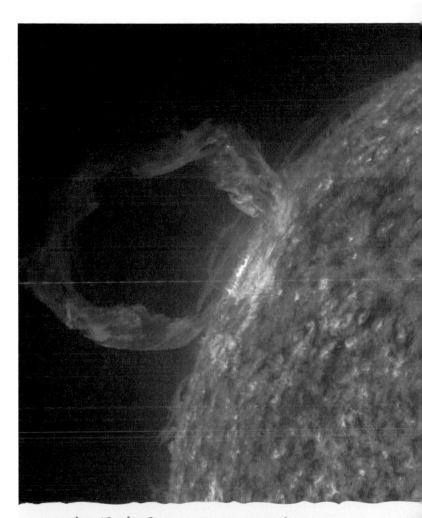

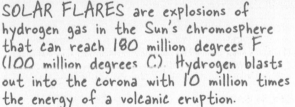

SOLAR FLARES are explosions of hydrogen gas in the Sun's chromosphere that can reach 180 million degrees F (100 million degrees C). Hydrogen blasts out into the corona with 10 million times the energy of a volcanic eruption.

hour (113 kph) and set it on cruise control for the whole ride, 24/7. At that speed, if no one stopped to get a bite of food or to take a bathroom break and the drivers rotated so that you never had to slow down or stop, you would arrive at the Sun **in 152 years!** How long is that? If your family had begun such a journey back in 1861 — the first year of the U.S. Civil War — you would finally reach your destination in 2013.

Even from that great distance, it takes the Sun's energy only 8 minutes and 20 seconds to reach us on Earth while traveling at the speed of light — around 670,000,000 miles (1,078,231,000 km) per hour. Traveling at that speed, sunlight would get a hefty speeding ticket on the interplanetary highway, if only someone could catch it!

How big is the Sun? It would take 109 Earths, placed edge to edge, to reach across the face of the Sun. And if you had a bag as large as the Sun, you could fit 1 million Earths inside.

A REAL BALL OF FIRE

At times, when a person is being very active, someone will say, "You're a regular ball of fire." But no one can hold a candle to the Sun. At its center or *core,* the Sun's temperature is 28 million °F (15.6 million °C). At this great heat the *atoms of hydrogen* join together to form *helium,* after the Greek name for the Sun, Helios. Energy is created every time hydrogen joins to form helium. This is the force that drives the Sun's energy. Even though 600 million tons (544,311,000 metric tons) of hydrogen change into helium every second, there is still enough hydrogen left for the Sun to last another 5 to 6 billion years.

When we catch a brief glimpse of the Sun, we see the 200-mile- (322 km) thick layer called the *photosphere,* which is about 10,000°F (5,500°C). *Sunspots* are areas that are cooler than the rest of the photosphere, so they appear darker. Some sunspots are wider than the diameter of Earth. They can last for anywhere from a few hours to a couple of months, and they can produce violent explosions called *solar flares.* A large solar flare can last for a few hours, interrupt satellite communications on Earth, and generate enough energy to **power the entire United States for 100,000 years.** Sunspot activity runs in cycles of about 11 years. A high point in the number of sunspots is expected from late 2011 through 2013.

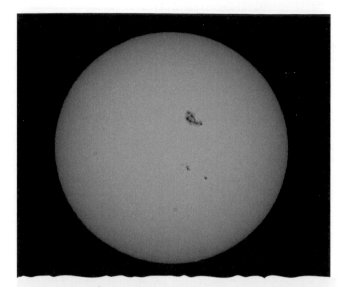

Sunspots form where colossal magnetic storms churn on the Sun's surface. Their temperature can reach 7,640°F (4,226°C) and they can grow to be four times the diameter of Earth.

FISSION VERSUS FUSION: CLEARING THE CONFUSION

The Sun's nuclear reaction, during which hydrogen atoms join to form helium atoms, is an example of *nuclear fusion.* During fusion, atoms with a small nucleus join to form an atom with a larger nucleus and release an enormous amount of energy.

Nuclear power plants employ *nuclear fission* — splitting atoms of uranium to generate heat for boiling water. This process also creates dangerous radioactive wastes, some of which have to be stored for millions of years before their radioactivity breaks down. There are 104 nuclear power plants in the United States and 20 in Canada.

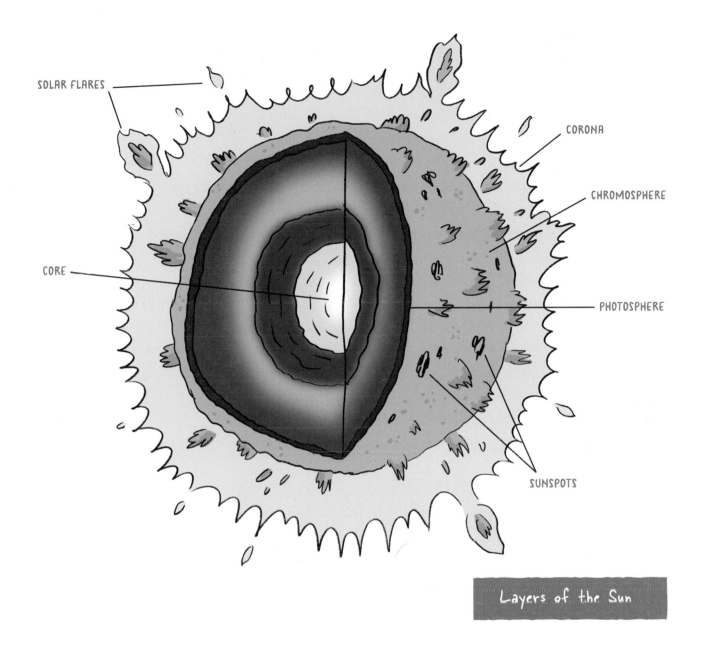

SOLAR FLARES

CORONA

CHROMOSPHERE

CORE

PHOTOSPHERE

SUNSPOTS

Layers of the Sun

Surrounding the photosphere is another, somewhat hotter layer of the Sun called the *chromosphere,* which is 1,000 to 2,000 miles (1,600 to 3,200 km) thick.

Finally, like a shimmering halo, comes the *corona,* in which the temperature shoots up to more than 1 million °F (555,500°C). Superheated gases from the corona rocket off into space as charged particles called the *solar wind.* We can only see the reddish chromosphere and the corona's whitish streamers during a *total solar eclipse,* a time when the moon passes directly between the Sun and Earth and the Sun is completely blocked out wherever the moon's shadow falls. But the Sun's energy can damage eyes and cause blindness, **so don't ever look directly at the Sun, even during an eclipse.**

NEON IN THE SKY

In the Northern Hemisphere, especially when sunspot activity is high, look for spectacular, shimmering displays of the **northern lights, Aurora Borealis.** In the Southern Hemisphere, catch the **southern lights, Aurora Australis.**

These dramatic nighttime spectacles are created when the solar wind sends charged *electrons* and *protons* (see Atomic Planets and the Charge Electric, on page 87) racing toward Earth, where they slide along Earth's magnetic field toward the North and South poles. There the solar particles crash into the molecules of Earth's atmospheric gases, causing those electrons to jump out of their orbits. The energy given off by the excited electrons shows up as brightly colored curtains and ribbons of light — green, red, pink, white, and lavender — in the skies over the polar regions.

We've all experienced or seen in books the brightly colored *neon lights* that spell out the names of city restaurants and markets. The process that creates the northern and southern lights is similar to the way a neon light works: Electricity passes through glass tubes filled with gas and causes the gas to glow. Each gas emits a different kind of color when it glows, such as neon (reddish orange), mercury (bright blue), argon (lavender), krypton (silver-white), xenon (pale blue), and helium (gold).

The northern lights are brightly colored curtains and ribbons aglow in the skies over the polar regions.

ATOMIC PLANETS AND THE CHARGE ELECTRIC

What's in a name? In the case of electricity, the source is in the name. **Electricity** is the flow of electrons.

Our Sun is circled by planets. That's **outer space**. The **inner space** of the elements all around us and inside us is composed of tiny units called **atoms**. Although they're far too small to see, about 100 years ago scientists began to create models showing how atoms might appear.

Picture the planet Saturn and imagine that its rings mark the path of an electron flowing quickly around the planet. Now imagine several other rings (electrons) at different angles to each other, and that's how some early models portrayed atoms. The center of each atom consists of a **nucleus** that makes up almost all of the mass of the atom and contains **protons** (which have a positive charge) and **neutrons** (which don't carry a charge). (If an atom were as big as a football field, the nucleus would be the size of a mosquito.)

Surrounding the nucleus in areas called **orbitals** are much lighter particles called **electrons**, which have negative charges and almost no mass. If a source of energy causes the electrons to become excited enough, they may leave their orbitals and separate from their atoms. When we catch these excited electrons and channel them to flow along a length of wire, we create a current that could be called "electron-icity," but it's known as electricity.

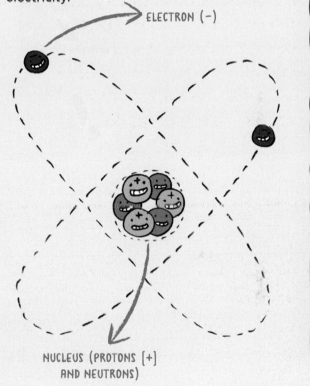

ELECTRON (−)

NUCLEUS (PROTONS [+] AND NEUTRONS)

SUN BURNS

If you ever wanted proof of the power of the Sun, the next set of activities is for you. By gathering the Sun's energy that falls over just a few inches of Earth's surface and focusing it with a magnifying glass, you can create a point of light-heat that is hot enough to light a fire with paper and even burn wood. The temperature at which something will burn is called the **flash point**. The flash point for paper is 451°F (233°C) and for wood is 572°F (300°C).

WRITING WITH SUNLIGHT

You will be amazed by the strength of the Sun's energy.

WHEN **WRITING WITH SUNLIGHT,** YOU'LL SEE HOW QUICKLY THE SUN BURNS INTO A PIECE OF WOOD TO CREATE A NAME PLATE OR SIGN. THEN YOU CAN PONDER HOW ELSE TO PUT THE SUN'S ENERGY TO USE.

! SAFETY FIRST !

Do this activity only with adult supervision. Wear safety glasses and work carefully when sawing wood. When using the magnifying glass, don't point the light anywhere but at the exact spot where you need it to focus for your activity. The magnifying glass focuses the Sun's powerful radiation to a tiny point that is extremely hot and bright. Use that point of sunlight with the same safety measures you would use when handling a lighted match.

Wear sunscreen that blocks UVA and UVB rays (SPF 30 minimum).

Wear sunglasses when looking at the focused point of sunlight. Use sunglasses that protect your eyes from 100 percent of the Sun's harmful ultraviolet rays, including UVA and UVB. Just to be safe, work on your Writing with Sunlight project for only short periods of 10 to 15 minutes per day, to give your eyes a long rest from looking at the bright light. If you do not wear sunglasses while doing this activity, or even while looking over the shoulder of someone else doing it, *you can burn your eyes' retinas.*

WHAT YOU WILL NEED

* UVA and UVB sunscreen (SPF 30 minimum)
* Flat piece of softwood such as white pine (a piece that is ½ inch [1.25 cm] thick by 4 inches [10 cm] wide will do); be sure it's long enough to fit the lettering you plan to use
* Safety goggles
* Small handsaw
* Sandpaper (medium grit, #80)
* Pencil
* Sunglasses (100% UVA & UVB protective)
* Handheld magnifying glass
* Eraser

DO THE DEED

All you need is a little patience and a steady hand to write with sunlight. Keep the point of the beam as small as possible, and use it like a hot pencil.

1 Decide what you want the sign to say. Perhaps you want to make a sign with your name or the name of a friend, a family member, or a pet. You could create a sign to hang on the door of your room. Or how about making a sign that says "Catch the Wind" or "Harness the Sun"?

2 Select a piece of wood for your sign. Any kind of wood will work, but softwoods, like white pine, are lightweight and easy to cut, sand, and burn. If you don't have a piece lying around the workshop in your house, go to a hardware store or lumberyard and ask if they have a short piece of scrap wood that they'll sell or give to you.

3

Put on your safety goggles and use the saw to cut the wood into the size and shape you want, being sure to allow enough room for some lettering. A single name would easily fit onto a piece that's about 12 inches (30 cm) long.

4 Sand the edges smooth so that the sign will look finished and you won't get splinters when handling the wood.

5

Using a pencil, lightly write the lettering onto the wood. Use simple block letters that are only a few inches high, and space them as you normally would when writing on paper.

6 Take the board outside on the next sunny day. Put on sunglasses to protect your eyes from the bright light. **(See the !Safety First! message about sunglasses at the beginning of this activity.)**

7 Use the magnifying glass to focus the sunbeam onto the first letter of your sign until it starts to smoke and turn black.

Gradually move the beam along the lines of the lettering, allowing the light to linger just long enough to create a black line where the Sun is burning into the wood. You are writing with sunlight!

9

Erase any leftover pencil marks so that your sign is Green and clean.

THE BIGGER PICTURE

THINK ABOUT IT

⊘ Can you think of any other small-scale tasks you could do or things you could make by focusing the sunlight in this way?

THINK HARDER

⊘ Now, think big. How could the Sun's heat energy be focused on a larger scale to create electricity? Keep in mind that enough heat would have to be gathered to boil water and create steam to turn the blades of a turbine that is connected to an electrical generator. Draw a diagram of how you could accomplish this by designing a solar electrical generator.

NOW, REALLY THINK

⊘ Once you've drawn your design, go online and search under "solar thermal plant" to see if the designs of real power stations are anything like the one you imagined.

SOLAR CAMPFIRE

Use the Sun's rays to start your campfire. Toast some marshmallows, grill some hot dogs, and warm yourself by the fire, all without burning any fossil fuels!

WHEN MAKING A SOLAR CAMPFIRE, YOU'LL SEE HOW EASY IT IS TO CREATE YOUR OWN HEAT SOURCE USING THE POWER OF THE SUN.

WHAT YOU WILL NEED

* Rocks to create a firebreak

* Tinder (newspaper or paper bags will work)

* Kindling and logs to lay for a fire, the drier the better

* Sunglasses (UVA and UVB protective)

* Handheld magnifying glass

* Something tasty to roast over your Solar Campfire

! SAFETY FIRST !

Get adult help and supervision with every step of creating a Solar Campfire. The magnifying glass focuses the Sun's powerful radiation to a tiny point that is extremely hot and bright. Don't point the light anywhere but on tinder. Use the same safety measures you would use when handling a lighted match.

Wear sunglasses that protect your eyes from 100 percent of the sun's harmful ultraviolet rays (UVA and UVB) when looking at the focused point of sunlight. To be safe, don't look at the point of sunlight for more than 10 to 15 minutes per day, to give your eyes a long rest. If you do not wear sunglasses, even while looking over the shoulder of another doing the activity, *you can burn your eyes' retinas.*

DO THE DEED

It doesn't take long to create heat with a point of sunlight. As soon as it strikes the tinder, it will begin to smoke. When you start your first campfire using sunlight instead of matches, you'll have to admit that this activity is really hot.

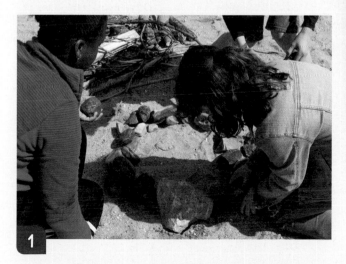

Lay out your fire in a pyramid shape. Place tinder, such as newspaper, a torn paper bag, or dry shredded tree bark, on the bottom. Layer the kindling (small sticks) on top of that, then add larger sticks and place a few small logs on top.

1 Gather large rocks and lay them out in a tight circle big enough to contain your largest logs.

3 Put on the sunglasses to shield your eyes from the intensity of the focused beam of sunlight.

Hold a handheld magnifying glass about 6 inches (15 cm) from the tinder. Move the magnifying glass closer or farther away until the light becomes a tiny point touching the tinder.

Focus the point of light on the tinder under some small kindling and keep it focused there. In a few seconds, the tinder will start to smoke, then smolder. **Don't let the beam of sunlight touch your skin or eyes or you will get burned.**

When it really begins to smoke heavily, blow gently on the ember that has started to glow until it bursts into flame.

7

Add more logs to stoke the fire as needed. Be careful to leave space underneath so that air can move through to feed the flames. Eventually, the fire will die down and form a bed of glowing coals.

THE BIGGER PICTURE

Does the size of your magnifying glass matter? Try different-sized magnifying lenses to see if the time it takes to start a fire changes.

THINK ABOUT IT

- ⊘ What kind of energy are you focusing to make things burn?

- ⊘ After the Sun has gone down, you may use the campfire for other kinds of activities that meet your needs. Has solar-powered fire helped you cook your supper? Warm your bodies? Heat your tea?

- ⊘ Create a campfire song about using the Sun's rays to power your camping fun after dark.

CHAPTER 8

SUN AND WIND

"Here comes the sun, and i say it's all right."

— The Beatles

Every single hour, enough of the Sun's energy reaches Earth to supply all of humankind's energy needs for an entire year. And that's just the beginning.

Heat created by the Sun warms the atmosphere. But Earth's surface has varied **terrain** — mountains and oceans, lakes, deserts, and forests — so warming occurs unevenly over its surface. When air is warmed, the molecules expand and take up more space, so the air weighs less, and it rises (this is why hot-air balloons are able to lift off). Cooler, heavier air then rushes in beneath the rising warmer air to take its place. These moving air masses, which are driven by the Sun's energy, are what we call **wind**. So **wind power is really another form of Sun power.**

As warm air rises higher into the atmosphere, it grows colder. When the temperature cools down to the **dew point** (the temperature at which water vapor condenses out of the air), the moisture forms tiny droplets that we see as **clouds**. This is also why we can see our breath when we exhale on a cold day. When enough moisture builds up in a cloud, it falls as rain. The building up of moisture in the air and the falling of rain, which happens over and over again, is called the **water cycle.** Sunshine is the engine that drives the water cycle.

Rain flows into streams and rivers, which empty out into lakes, ponds, and the ocean, so when the power of flowing water is captured behind a dam and used to generate electricity, what is the ultimate source of that power? Right . . . the Sun!

A SUN-POWERED FACTORY

Sunshine feeds the life force of every green growing plant on Earth. Its light energy powers the quadrillions of tiny food factories we call leaves, which use sunlight to manufacture sugars, starches, and other forms of food for plants. And all these plants are watered by rain, which was formed and driven by the Sun.

ALL DRIED UP

Clothes dryers may sometimes shrink your clothes, but they cause your carbon footprint to grow. When it comes to energy consumption, clothes dryers are "all wet."

Did you know that a clothes dryer is one of the biggest energy hogs? An average household uses about 931 kilowatt hours of energy each year to dry clothes. How much is that? When multiplied by the number of U.S. households (106 million), this comes out to 98,686 gigawatt hours that we use in the United States each year to dry our clothes. An average coal-fired power plant in the United States produces 3,400 gigawatt hours of electricity each year.

How could your family easily conserve 931 kilowatt hours of electricity each year? Why, by using the Sun and its friend the wind, of course (see the activity on page 100).

Let's do the math:

98,686 gigawatt hours (total used by dryers in U.S.) ÷ 3,400 gigawatt hours (average output of coal-fired power plants in U.S.) = 29

That's how many coal-fired power plants are needed to create enough energy just to dry our clothes!

Watt's Watt?

1 kilowatt	= 1,000 watts
1 megawatt	= 1,000,000 watts
1 gigawatt	= 1,000,000,000 watts

GREEN GIANT

COLIN CARLSON, COVENTRY, CONNECTICUT

COOL DUDE

"I've always loved nature," says Colin Carlson. "When I was nine I visited the Galápagos Islands as part of the first-ever National Geographic Kids' Expedition Team. While visiting a beach known for its waddles of Galápagos penguins, I was shocked to discover only five of these special birds. I learned that this decline was due to an increasingly frequent El Niño (foul weather) pattern caused by global warming and promised myself and the penguins to do something when I got home to help the historic treasure that is the Galápagos.

"Climate change is definitely the most important environmental issue we face today," he says. "If we don't get climate change under control, we aren't going to be able to fix the other problems . . . period."

Colin's Galápagos experience planted the seed for the Cool Coventry Club, the ambitious project that he designed for helping people in his hometown of Coventry, Connecticut, to think globally and act locally. "I decided when I was ten to launch a project to educate people in my own town and elsewhere in the United States about the causes of global warming and the steps necessary to reduce it; I named my organization the Cool Coventry Club (CCC), both because I want to keep our climate cool and because I wanted to express that it's 'cool' to fight global warming," he explains.

A Blueprint for Change

"First, I researched the changes that are working in other communities to eliminate global warming and solutions," says Colin. "I also studied the psychology of behavior change, so that I could advocate effectively. Then I based my plan on what I learned."

Next came the detailed planning behind every successful program, even those born of inspiration. Colin contacted his local church, town library, town hall, and supermarket to get permission for hosting CCC events. Then, he says, "I found experts to make presentations and canvassed businesses to partner with me by advertising and attending events; developing action plans to reduce energy use; and donating funds, goods, and services.

"I launched an energy-reduction Pledge Campaign on my website [see Resources]. Then I collected printed information to pass out at tabling events, such as clean-energy enrollment forms; catalogs of energy-saving products; my own 'Things You Can Do' sheets; energy-conservation magnets and stickers; and pamphlets about global warming, cleaner cars, state energy programs, solar-power products, and 'biobricks' (carbon-neutral sawdust heating bricks made in my state that are more efficient than cordwood).

"Later, I began making presentations to school and teacher groups, created a 16-page booklet for elementary students, wrote newspaper articles, and spoke on the radio about climate change."

In its first few years, the CCC has hosted over 50 events throughout Connecticut and in three other states, reaching more than 2,000 people. Colin led petition drives that convinced his hometown to obtain 20 percent of its energy from carbon-neutral sources by 2010, and that

> ## "DON'T LET ANYONE TELL YOU THAT YOU CAN'T MAKE A DIFFERENCE, BECAUSE EVEN TEN-YEAR-OLDS CAN CHANGE THEIR COMMUNITIES, AND THE WORLD."

enabled the CCC to install recycling bins in local parks. The CCC has distributed — both free and at cost — hundreds of energy-saving compact fluorescent lightbulbs. Participants in the CCC Pledge Campaign receive rewards like KEEP COVENTRY COOL! bumper stickers, canvas bags, and homemade reusable shopping bags donated by a local supermarket and Home Depot. Finally, in 2008, Colin's work was recognized in a big way when he won the International Eco-Hero Award from Action For Nature.

Colin's work through the CCC succeeds because he networks and builds business partnerships. He now has about 70 individual and business partners and has partnered with the Connecticut Fund for the Environment and the Sierra Club by testifying in front of the state legislature.

A Strong Following

Colin's town, and many local residents, now participates in Connecticut's Clean Energy Option program. Customers who sign up pay extra to support renewable energy made from solar, wind, and small-scale hydropower.

"Coventry has even won a free solar panel system and windmill from the state, to honor the progress we have made. Four years ago, I never would have imagined that was possible," Colin exclaims.

The motto of the Cool Coventry Club is **One person can make a difference — I can, and so can you.** "Don't let anyone tell you that you can't make a difference," says Colin, "because even ten-year-olds can change their communities, and the world. Don't wait for other people to take the lead. If you can think of an activity that would be helpful, start working on it today."

Colin now balances his work at the CCC with his studies in college, which he began at age twelve. He is an honors student at the University of Connecticut working on two degrees (B.A., B.S.) in environmental studies and ecology and environmental biology.

DRYING CLOTHES ON-LINE

By hanging your clothes to dry outside instead of using a dryer, your family will use less electricity and cut down your carbon footprint.

AFTER DRYING CLOTHES ON-LINE, USE THE FORMULA AT THE END OF THE ACTIVITY TO SEE EXACTLY HOW MUCH ENERGY YOU COULD HAVE SAVED.

WHAT YOU WILL NEED

* Clothesline
* Supports that are about 20 feet (6 m) apart on which to tie the ends of the clothesline, such as two trees or porch columns
* Rope, if necessary

* Two eye hooks, to tie the ends of the rope onto if necessary
* Bag of clothespins
* Paper
* Pen
* Calculator

DO THE DEED

If you strung a clothesline and put up a sign that said "Free clothes-drying service. Just hang them here," do you think anyone would use it? Try it yourself, and see how it works.

1 Find a place to hang a clothesline; a sunny place is best. This could be a space between your house or apartment and a nearby tree or swing set. It could stretch between two trees, or you could stretch the line across a porch between two columns. If you do attach it to a tree, tie a loop of rope around the tree, then knot your clothesline onto that rope. (Please don't nail or screw anything into the tree. Tree bark is like our skin — once broken, it is open to infections that can sicken and eventually kill the tree.)

2 String the clothesline snugly between the two hanging points.

3 Use clothespins to hang your clothes and dry them "on-line." This is an old-fashioned, low-tech solution to a major environmental issue. And your clothes will smell great!

THE BIGGER PICTURE

People have been drying their garments out in the Sun and wind for as long as they've been wearing clothes. But they may not have thought about it.

THINK ABOUT IT

- How long did it take for your clothes and towels to dry?

- Did some dry quicker than others? If so, why?

- Do you think some buildings and spaces get warmer or cooler faster than other buildings and spaces? If so, why?

- Watch to see if your clothes dry faster when the wind is blowing or when it is calm. When do they dry faster? Why do you think this is so?

THINK HARDER

- How much energy would you save by drying your clothes on a line?

2.6* kilowatt hours/day (about) x _____ (days per year your clothes dry on-line)

= _____ kilowatt hours saved per year

* 931 kilowatt hours of electricity can be saved each year by always drying clothes on-line.

931 ÷ 365 days per year = 2.6

- Come up with a clothes-hanging schedule that you, your parents, and your siblings can all agree to. Remind them that you can all work together to help the planet stay healthy. Tape the schedule next to the door closest to the line, and when the wash is done, invite a brother, sister, parent, or friend to have a clothes-hanging race out in the sunshine.

NOW, REALLY THINK

Every year it takes 29 coal-fired power plants to power just the clothes dryers in the United States. An average coal plant in the United States emits more than 3.5 million tons (3.2 million metric tons) of carbon dioxide into the atmosphere each year.

- How many millions of tons of carbon emissions would the United States put a stop to by letting our clothes dry in the Sun and wind?

CHAPTER 9

RENEWABLE, EVERY DAY

"Give me the splendid silent sun, with all his beams full-dazzling!"

— Walt Whitman, *Leaves of Grass*

Oil, coal, and natural gas, also called *fossil fuels,* were formed from the remains of prehistoric plants fed by sunlight, plus the animals that ate those plants. That means fossil fuel is solar power stored underground from sunlight that shone long ago. These kinds of energy took millions of years to form, and **it will take another few million years to make more.** So when we rely on fossil fuels to heat our houses and run our cars, we are counting on types of energy that will one day run out. Once fossil fuels are all taken out of the ground, there won't be any more for millions of years.

The Sun, however, shines every day, so its energy won't run out. Even on cloudy days when the Sun doesn't "come out," our home star is up there wrapping Earth in its powerful blanket of energy. That's why solar energy is called *renewable* — it sustains itself constantly, which means it will give us life and won't run out for at least another 5 billion years.

SUNWISE

The Sun is our guiding star. It shapes our lives. When some big, new event is about to begin, we say it is "the dawn of a new day." In literature, people often meet "at high noon," for better or for worse. And at the end of the day, heroes and heroines "ride off into the sunset."

Time itself was once measured with *sundials,* which tracked the movement of a shadow cast by the Sun. Today's clocks, too, are related to the Sun's movements. If you are standing in the Northern Hemisphere (north of the equator) and facing south, you'll notice that the sun moves from left to right as it travels across the sky.

When mechanical clocks were invented, in England, the hands of the first clock were made to mirror the direction that the Sun moves across the sky. Today we call this direction *clockwise,* but some indigenous peoples still refer to it as *sunwise.*

The design for a modern sundial, like the one above, was invented by Islamic cultures during early Medieval times.

Even though the Sun has so much positive potential, we use solar energy for only a tiny amount of our energy supply. **Just 7 percent of our energy comes from all renewable sources put together,** including solar, wind, hydroelectric, tidal, geothermal, and biomass power (see the box on page 105). But only 1 percent of this 7 percent comes from solar power! That means less than $\frac{1}{10}$ of 1 percent of our total energy supply comes from the Sun. That's a tiny amount!

The Sun doesn't care where it falls or on whom its rays shine. The Sun reaches all places — high and low; wet and dry; tropical, temperate, and covered with snow and ice. Despite this abundance of sunshine, there are about 2 billion people in the world who still don't have electricity. It would cost less to power these households with solar energy than it would to create new power plants and power lines. There is a lot of potential for solar power. How can you help?

RENEWABLE ENERGY SOURCES

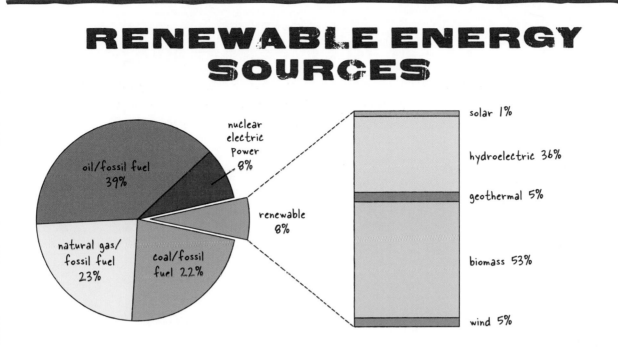

SOLAR POWER

The Sun's energy is used to heat water and buildings. It is also captured and converted into electricity using photovoltaic panels. Heat from the Sun is sometimes used to create rising hot air and steam, both of which can spin turbines to generate electricity.

WIND POWER

Wind is used to turn the blades of a windmill that are connected to a turbine. As the turbine spins, it generates electricity.

HYDROELECTRIC POWER

Falling or flowing water is captured by a waterwheel or by the blades of a turbine and used to spin a generator to create electricity.

TIDAL POWER

There are different ways to create electricity using tides, currents, and waves. Water that comes in during high tide is captured behind a dam; then it is run through chutes to spin turbines to generate electricity. In some places, where tides and ocean currents are strong enough, the natural movement of ocean water spins the turbines. The up-and-down motion of waves is also harnessed.

GEOTHERMAL POWER

One kind of geothermal energy uses pipes filled with water or antifreeze to capture the steady temperature that lies about 6 feet (2 m) underground, and below. This fluid is pumped up to the surface and used to cool buildings on hot summer days and to warm them during winter's chill.

Another form of geothermal energy uses wells that are drilled into Earth's crust to bring up superheated water that is used as steam to spin turbines for electricity.

BIOMASS ENERGY

Renewable power from plants and animals is called biomass energy. Stoves that heat by burning wood, wood pellets, and other plant matter are the most common use of biomass fuel. Wood is also burned in power plants to generate electricity. Some farms capture the methane that is given off when manure decomposes and burn it to create electricity. *Biodiesel* fuel is burned in diesel engines and in furnaces to heat buildings and hot water. It can be made from vegetable oils and even from used restaurant oil, which smells like French fries when it burns.

ACTIVITY

THAT'S SUN COOKIN'

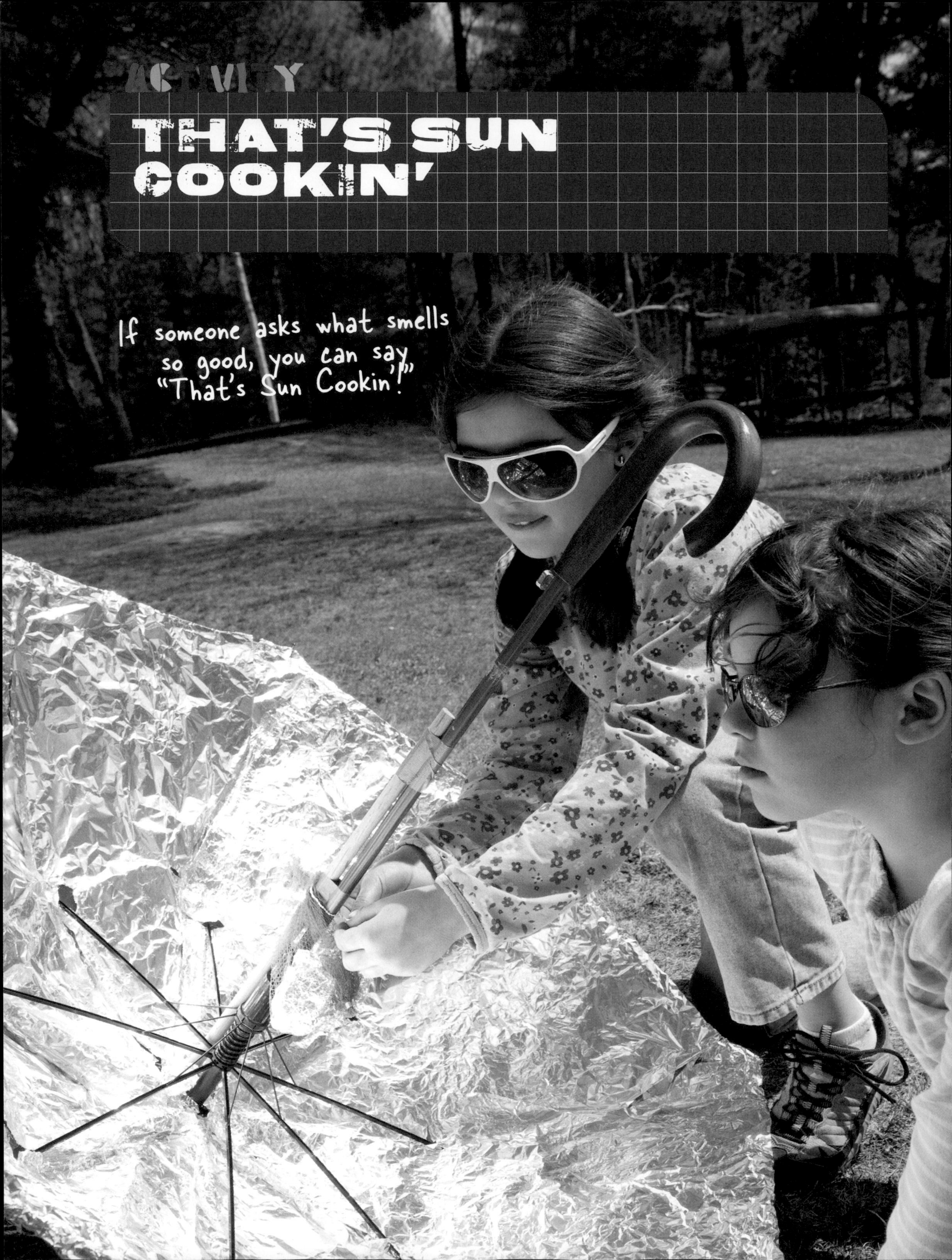

If someone asks what smells so good, you can say, "That's Sun Cookin'!"

HOW CAN YOU USE THE SUN'S ENERGY TO CREATE MORE OF YOUR MEALS? CREATE A SIMPLE, EASY-TO-MAKE "UMBRELLA" SOLAR COOKER USING THE FOLLOWING STEPS.

! SAFETY FIRST !

Be sure to have a parent or teacher on hand when using a knife to whittle the wood for this next experiment. As with all activities in the Sun — those in this book and those you partake in every day — wear UV-protective sunglasses to shield your eyes from ultraviolet rays, including UVA and UVB. Wear sunscreen that also blocks UVA abd UVB rays (SPF 30 minimum).

WHAT YOU WILL NEED

* UVA & UVB sunscreen (SPF 30 minimum)
* Old umbrella
* Aluminum foil
* Scissors
* Roll of clear tape
* Duct tape
* Pair of sunglasses (100% UVA & UVB protective)
* Permanent marker
* A 2-foot- (60 cm) long wooden dowel ½ inch (1.25 cm) wide
* Jackknife, for carving wood
* Onion, hot dog, veggie burger, or other food that can be wrapped
* Old, net-style onion bag
* Two long baggie twist ties

DO THE DEED

Be sure to try this during the warmer months rather than in the winter, when the Sun is relatively weak. It works best on days when the temperature is 75°F (24°C) or higher.

1 Open an old umbrella and place it on the floor or ground upside down, so the edges curl up.

2 Roll out one sheet of aluminum foil that is long enough to reach from the center of the umbrella to about 3 inches (8 cm) past the outer edge. Be sure to press down the foil along the curve of the umbrella before you cut. It needs to be long enough so that in the next step you can use it to form the bowl shape inside the umbrella. Cut this piece to length with the scissors.

3 Place the piece of foil inside the umbrella and mold it to cover one of the sections between ribs, so it is shaped like a piece of pie. You'll need to cut a slit on each side so that the foil will fit around the supports sticking up inside the umbrella. Now run your finger gently along the foil over the two ribs that make the pie shape. Carefully remove the piece so you can still see where the ribs made an impression on the foil.

4 Cut out this triangular-shaped piece, but leave about 2 inches (5 cm) extra beyond the rib mark on each side. This piece is going to be your pattern for tracing all the other pieces.

5 Count the number of pie-shaped sections that make up the whole umbrella. Lay the pattern piece over a larger piece of foil. Cut around the edge of the pattern piece. Repeat this until you have enough triangles to cover all the sections in the opened umbrella. These foil pieces will become the lining of the cooker's reflector.

6 Tape a triangular (pie-shaped) piece of foil into each section of the umbrella to create a mirrorlike lining over the entire inside surface. Use clear tape to secure the long sides of foil onto the ribs inside the umbrella. Fold the outer edge of foil around the outside rim of the umbrella and fasten with duct tape.

Use the pieces of foil that were trimmed off to fill in any sections inside the umbrella that are not yet lined with foil. Try to keep the foil as wrinkle-free as possible to best reflect the sunlight.

7 On the next sunny day, put on a pair of sunglasses and take your budding solar cooker outside for some fine-tuning. Place it in a sunny spot out of the wind, with the reflective side facing the Sun. Turn it so the handle is pointing exactly at the Sun.

8 Wait a few minutes, then feel the place on the handle that is the hottest. This is the point where the reflected sunlight is strongest. *Be careful because the handle can become very hot.* Mark this spot with a permanent marker. With most umbrellas, this zone will be about 10 to 14 inches (25–35 cm) up from the place where the shaft of the umbrella handle attaches to the crown.

9 Before you begin, be sure an adult is helping with this step! Use the jackknife to whittle the end of the dowel to a sharp point. Point the knife blade away from your body while you whittle.

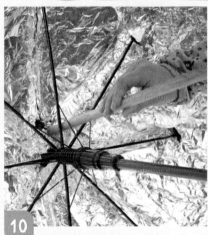

10 Line up the dowel with the umbrella handle, with the sharp tip pointing toward the ground. Using gentle pressure, twist the point of the dowel like a drill until it makes a hole through the umbrella cloth as close to the pole as possible. Continue to push the point of the dowel down, into the ground about 6 inches (15 cm), so it is firmly anchoring the umbrella-cooker. Use a few pieces of duct tape to fasten the dowel to the pole.

11 Tightly seal the food you want to cook in two layers of aluminum foil, so it doesn't drip as it cooks. Use enough foil to be able to completely enclose the food, folding the foil over it several times. Twist the long, folded, loose foil ends together on top of the package.

12

Put the sealed food into the onion bag and close the top with a twist tie. Use the other twist tie to fasten the top of the onion bag to the pole so the food is attached right next to the mark you made where the reflected sunlight is the hottest. Keep the twist tie from slipping by wrapping it with a small piece of duct tape.

13 As the food cooks, the Sun will keep changing location. Adjust the angle of the solar cooker every 20 minutes to keep the tip of the center pole facing the Sun.

14 The actual cooking time will depend on the kind of food you're cooking and the angle of the Sun in your location at that time of year.

THE BIGGER PICTURE

Don't let your solar-cooking experience be half-baked. Finish with a course of exercise for the brain.

THINK ABOUT IT

- Try making other kinds of reflective solar cookers out of similarly shaped bases, such as a wok; an old, saucer-shaped snow sled; or even a large old salad bowl. With these bases, you'll have to create a small stand in the center to lift the food to the *focal point* of the Sun's energy — the spot where the heat is being concentrated. You can fashion this out of a sturdy dowel fastened with a screw at the bottom or secured to a piece of wood, but make sure that the stand doesn't interfere with the sunlight reflecting in from the mirrored bowl.

- Create a "Bernard Solar Panel Cooker" from a cardboard box, a design that is easy to make and transport. (Designs can be found online.)

THINK HARDER

- Make a tin-can oven to hang in your solar cooker. First, clean a medium-sized soup can and cover the outside with black construction paper. Position the can so that the center (measuring from top to bottom) rests next to the mark showing where the umbrella shaft becomes hottest. Attach by wrapping two pieces of masking tape around both the can and the shaft of the umbrella. Place your food inside the can and cover it with a lid or piece of aluminum foil.

- Look around your neighborhood, school, and beyond for other kinds of structures and electronic devices that are shaped like your solar cooker: a curved bottom with some kind of sensor located at the focal point. Can you find any? (Hint: Think BIG!) In the case of these devices, what is sitting at the focal point, and what kind of energy or information is it gathering?

NOW, REALLY THINK

⊘ Use some simple math (algebra) to locate precisely the hottest point in the center of your solar cooker. Do this by calculating the focal point of the curved surface of your umbrella, which forms a shape that is called a *parabola*. Here's how:

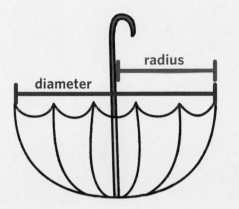

1 Measure the farthest distance straight across the center of the umbrella, from side to side. This is the *diameter*. We'll imagine this is 48 inches (122 cm).

2 Divide the diameter in half to get the *radius*: 48 ÷ 2 = 24 inches (122 ÷ 2 = 61 cm)

3 Square the radius: 24 × 24 = 576 inches (61 × 61 = 3,721 cm)

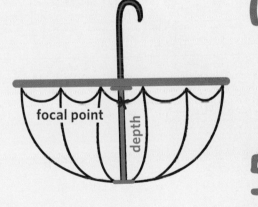

4 Measure the depth of the umbrella/parabola in the center. To do this, set a straight edge, such as a thin piece of wood, across the mouth of the open umbrella, passing through the center. Then measure how far down it is from the straight edge to the deepest part of the curve in the center. We'll say this measurement is 13 inches (33 cm).

5 Multiply the depth by 4: 13 × 4 = 52 inches (33 × 4 = 132 cm)

6 Divide the square of the radius by this last number to get the focal point: 576 ÷ 52 = 11 inches (3,721 ÷ 132 = 28 cm)

The *focal point* — the hottest place inside this solar cooker — would be 11 inches (28 cm) up the umbrella handle from where it attaches to the crown of the umbrella.

SUN TEA

An old song says, "Tea for two, and two for tea." In many parts of the world, tea is a social drink that brings people together.

BREW SOME SUN TEA AND INVITE YOUR FRIENDS OVER FOR A "GREEN" TEA PARTY WHERE YOU USE ONLY RENEWABLE SOURCES OF ENERGY.

WHAT YOU WILL NEED

* Eight tea bags, caffeinated only
* One ½-gallon (2 L) clean glass jar full of drinking water
* Cups and teaspoons
* Optional: a bit of honey and a sprig of fresh mint

! SAFETY FIRST !

Wash hands and containers thoroughly with hot, soapy water before making Sun Tea, then store the tea in the refrigerator in order to prevent bacteria from growing. Don't store the tea for very long; make small batches that you and your family and friends will drink within a day. Use caffeinated tea, which helps prevent bacteria from growing.

DO THE DEED

You can use any tea, but green tea is nice because it is especially healthful and its name symbolizes doing something good for our Earth. It has a light flavor and is rich in nutrients that keep your body healthy, including such vitamins as A, B, D, H, and K, as well as vitamins C and E and other antioxidants — chemicals that protect your cells.

1 Drop the tea bags into the jar and fill it with cool drinking water. Cap the jar.

2 Place the jar in direct sunlight for about 2 hours, or until the water becomes brightly colored. On warm days, the jar can go outside in a protected, sunny place. If it's cool outside, place the jar in a sunny window indoors. Don't steep the tea for more than two hours.

3 Once the tea has taken on a rich color, uncap the jar and pull out the tea bags. Serve the tea warm and fresh, and, if you like, with a few leaves of fresh mint and a touch of honey. Or chill and serve as iced tea. Store in the refrigerator.

THE BIGGER PICTURE

⊘ **Did you know? In China, green tea is used to prevent headaches, ease depression, improve energy, and keep the heart healthy.**

CHAPTER 10

CAPTURE THE SUN

"Keep your face to the sunshine."

— Helen Keller

ike a wild bronco, the Sun's energy is all over the place. **But we can tame that energy and put it to work.** There are several ways to do this.

Simply catching the rays of the Sun is called *passive solar.* Passive solar is used in three ways: (1) to heat a house or other space; (2) to heat water; and (3) to bring light into dark spaces.

PASSIVE SOLAR HEAT

To heat spaces or water with passive solar, all you need is a sunny window or something dark to absorb solar heat. The darker the color, the more of the Sun's energy it absorbs. Spaces can be solar-heated by building them with large, south-facing, insulated windows for catching and holding the heat. If the walls and floors are a dark color where the sun

WITH THE RIGHT KIND OF EQUIPMENT, IT'S POSSIBLE TO USE SUNLIGHT TO CREATE ELECTRICITY.

Solar collectors catch the energy of the Sun to heat water in a home even on cold winter days.

strikes, they will absorb solar heat during the day and radiate that same heat into the house at night. Some people keep large, often dark-colored containers of water in the sunlight. Once water heats up, it radiates that heat for a long time.

Many solar water heaters consist of dark tubes that are enclosed in a glass-covered flat box, or panel, and exposed to the Sun. Fluid that runs through tubes is used to heat water. In some systems, the water is heated directly by the Sun. These *solar collectors* can be placed on a roof or on a raised platform in a sunny place on the ground. There are a lot of solar hot-water heaters already being used in North America, including those that are designed for heating pools.

PASSIVE SOLAR LIGHT

Some houses have interior rooms with no windows or dark rooms with small windows. Many times, with good planning, small daylight shafts, such as the *Solatube*, can be made to catch and direct light from a brightly lit part of a roof or wall down into the dark room. These shafts are either painted white or lined with a shiny metal surface to reflect the light down.

SUN-TRICITY

With the right kind of equipment, it's possible to use sunlight to generate electricity.

Photovoltaic, which means "electricity from light," comes from the Greek word for light (*phot-*) and the name of the Italian inventor Alessandro Volta, who created the first battery (see the brief history of Volta in chapter 16, on page 179).

Picture tiny **electrons** moving around the nucleus of an atom (see page 87). When the Sun's energy strikes a photovoltaic solar panel, which is usually made from an element called **silicon,** the electrons become energized. They escape their atomic bonds and can only move from bottom to top through the photovoltaic (PV) cell's two thin layers of silicon. (The lower section, which has too few electrons, is called the **positive [p-type] layer,** and the upper is the **negative [n-type] layer.**) Opposing charges on the top and bottom cause electrons to flow through the circuit of wires attached to the PV cell to form a **current.**

The electrons moving along the wire from the PV cell form **direct current,** or **DC.** This current can be used to power things that run on electricity or it can be stored in batteries for use later on. If someone wants to feed this power into a household electrical system, it is usually run through an inverter, which changes the DC current to **alternating current** or **AC** — which is what our household appliances are designed for.

Less than ½ of 1 percent of all the electricity that is generated in the world is made using photovoltaic panels. Isn't it time that we put more of the Sun's colossal power to work?

SUNLIGHT
(PHOTONS)

FLOWING ELECTRONS
= DC CURRENT

SILICON LAYERS

N-TYPE LAYER
P-TYPE LAYER

NEGATIVE
POSITIVE

The Sun's energy knocks electrons out of their atomic orbitals (see page 87). Electrons flow into the upper layer of silicon, then through the circuit of wires to produce a current.

CURRENT CHOICES

When you start to work with renewable energy, you'll soon discover these two terms: **AC (alternating current)** and **DC (direct current)**. Both terms describe how electrons flow while they're creating current. With DC, all the electrons flow in one direction. We could save some energy by powering more of our electronic devices using low-voltage DC current generated by Sun, wind, and crank power.

Alternating current flows back and forth in regular cycles. High-voltage AC is the energy carried for hundreds of miles along most of our power lines. We tap into AC every time we plug something into an electrical outlet. In the United States and Canada, AC cycles 60 times per second. Since one cycle consists of current flowing in both directions, this means that the current alternates or changes direction 120 times per second. These cycles happen so quickly that our lights don't even flicker.

➡ **ENERGY CAN BE SAVED BY USING LOW-VOLTAGE DC CURRENT GENERATED BY SUN, WIND, AND CRANK POWER.**

➡ **HIGH-VOLTAGE AC IS CARRIED FOR HUNDREDS OF MILES ALONG OUR POWER LINES.**

➡ **AC ALTERNATES OR CHANGES DIRECTION 120 TIMES PER SECOND.**

AC is used more often, but it's easy to produce your own DC current from renewable energy sources.

GREEN GIANT

MICHELLE MARCUS, VANCOUVER, BRITISH COLUMBIA

ONE SMART COOKIE

If you want to know what's cooking when it comes to the environment in British Columbia, then visit the Green and Clean Earth website (see Resources). One founder and major contributor is Michelle Marcus. From topics focused on saving electricity and making your own Green candles to pages that will help you learn about frogs, flowers, snowy owls, and the Vancouver Island marmot, the website contains an awesome range of information and activities. This young Earth advocate knows that the actions of local youth have an impact on the environment that reaches way beyond the emerald green shores of this strikingly beautiful Canadian province.

It all started when Michelle was nine years old and joined the school's environmental club, run by a dynamic teacher, Sharon Bool. "She really inspired me to make a difference in the world," says Michelle. "She made me aware that there are environmental problems in the world and showed me ways to decrease them. She showed us how to recycle and care for the planet."

One Project Leads to Another

Michelle got her activist start raising money for Pennies for Peace to build schools in Afghanistan and Pakistan. After her Pennies for Peace group got permission from the principal, says Michelle, "We spoke at assemblies, made posters, made announcements, and supplied each classroom with a bin to fill up with money. Then we rolled up all the money and found out that we had raised almost $2,000!"

But Michelle didn't stop there. She encouraged a hundred students and teachers to sign a schoolwide petition, then sent it to the premier of British Columbia, asking for legislation to protect endangered species in the province.

Like other Green Giants, encouragement at home has been a key to Michelle's successes. "My mom has supported and helped me with all of my projects. She supplies me with all the things I need and gives me ideas to make my projects succeed."

In turn, Michelle's drive has motivated others. And kids are discovering how it can also be fun to make a difference. They're baking up something sweet in their Green oven: ecofriendly cookie dough.

"We started a cookie club where we sell cookies that do not harm the environment," says Michelle. "We make organic cookie dough and package it with reused and biodegradable materials. My cookie project is very fun, but it also shows people how to make environmental choices — for example, buying organic food, things with less packaging, and things with environmental packaging."

The Bigger Picture

Baking may be fun when it involves cookies, but it's not when it's the planet that's getting cooked. Of all the environmental issues Earth now faces, Michelle believes that global warming is the most important. "There are many causes to global warming," she says. "Burning of fossil fuels creates CO_2, and the destruction of forests means that less carbon is taken out of the atmosphere. Global warming can cause serious climate change. Ice caps are melting, and animals are becoming endangered due to the intense climate. Clean-energy alternatives to fossil fuels and responsible management of our forests will decrease the impact of global warming."

How does Michelle find hope in the face all of this bad news? "There are many environmental problems in the world that need to be stopped," she says. "If everyone takes part and makes one small change, there will be a big difference in the world! I believe that anyone can change the world."

Michelle is definitely on to something. Not only is she feeding people's minds, she also understands that when it comes to taking care of Earth, one sure way to people's hearts is through their stomachs.

"IF **EVERYONE** TAKES PART AND **MAKES** ONE **SMALL CHANGE,** THERE WILL BE A **BIG DIFFERENCE** IN THE WORLD."

Michelle went green for Halloween.

SOLAR HEAT BY THE GALLON

A container of water that heats up in the sunlight during the day continues to give off that heat well into the night.

SOLAR HEAT BY THE GALLON ISN'T VERY DIFFICULT TO MAKE. FOLLOW THESE STEPS TO CREATE YOUR OWN SMALL PASSIVE–CAPTURE SOLAR HEATER.

WHAT YOU WILL NEED

* Dish soap

* Four (or more) 2-liter beverage bottles with screw-on lids

* Dish drainer

* Drop cloth

* Paintbrush

* Can of flat black interior latex paint (any flat, dark color will do)

* Clean, 1-liter container of water for cleaning paint brushes

* Water for filling bottles

! SAFETY FIRST !

Use only water-based latex paint. Spray paints are toxic if inhaled and they often contain chemicals made from petroleum. Do your painting outside in a well-ventilated space.

DO THE DEED

1 Use the dish soap to thoroughly clean all the plastic beverage bottles. Save the caps. Remove labels from the outside of the bottles and wash the outside well so the surface is clean and paint will stick to it. Rinse the inside of each container well and put it upside down in the dish drainer to dry.

2 Once the beverage containers are dry, place them on the drop cloth and paint with flat black paint. It is best to do this outside or in an open garage or other well-ventilated space.

3 Use the container of water for cleaning the paint brush, then set the brush aside to dry.

4 Once the paint is dry, fill each bottle with water. Put the caps on snugly, leaving about 1 inch (2.5 cm) of air on top to allow space for the water to expand as it warms up. Be sure not to crush or bend the containers while handling them or the paint might crack off.

5 Place the black jugs full of water on the top of a bookshelf in a sunny window or on a windowsill to create a simple solar heat collector.

THE BIGGER PICTURE

Now that you have your own personal heater, you can experiment with ways to get the most output and be even more efficient.

THINK ABOUT IT

- Add more shelves and "Solar Heat by the Gallon" jugs to your homemade heat collector to increase its storage capacity.

- Experiment by placing other kinds of dark-colored containers full of water in the Sun to see which one holds the heat longest once the Sun goes down. Try using containers made from glass, ceramic, metal, and thicker plastic. Which kind of container works best? Why?

THINK HARDER

- On a sunny day: Open one of the bottles of water in the morning and immerse a cooking thermometer or a science-class dial thermometer inside it. If the bottle is taller than the thermometer, you may need to tie a string around the top of the thermometer.

  Now make a graph showing the temperature along the left-hand side and the time along the bottom. Read the thermometer every half hour, capping the container after each reading. Use a dot to record the temperature at each half-hour time mark. Once the Sun goes down, observe how the temperature rose and fell during the day. When was the "heat of the day?" Was it exactly in the middle of the day? Why or why not?

  Try this same experiment by recording and graphing the water temperature on a cloudy day. How does this temperature pattern compare with the results from the sunny day?

NOW, REALLY THINK

- Repeat the previous experiment using two bottles: one that sits in direct sunlight and one that rests in the shade. Using a different-colored marker for each bottle, chart the temperature of both bottles on your graph throughout the day. Compare the temperature changes that occurred in each bottle. Why do you think you got that result? Is it what you expected?

  How does the temperature chart from the bottle that sat in the shade in this experiment compare with the graph you made earlier of the bottle kept exposed to the sky on a cloudy day?

CHAPTER 11

PLUGGING IN TO SUNLIGHT

"I'D PUT MY MONEY ON THE SUN AND SOLAR ENERGY. WHAT A SOURCE OF POWER!"

— Thomas Alva Edison, 1931

How would you like to have your own personal power station? Wouldn't it be outstanding to show your concern for Earth's health by creating clean, renewable energy from the Sun? Energy you can feel good about?

Catch the Wind, Harness the Sun is all about tapping in to renewable energy in a way that is simple and homemade or, if purchased, as inexpensive as possible. When it comes to catching the Sun's energy and using it for electricity, however, there are a few basic things you will need that you cannot make at home.

For less than the cost of an iPod or iPhone, you can:

- Set yourself up to catch sunlight with a small solar panel
- Store that charge in a battery
- Use the battery-stored charge for powering any 12-volt device

This, your Personal Solar Power (PSP), is especially good for charging those things you use all the time, like your laptop, your cell phone, and even your iPod! You can also use your PSP for powering a wide variety of 12-volt devices, such as a desk lamp, a fan, and a radio.

PERSONAL SOLAR POWER

You can listen to your favorite music or talk to your friends while doing the planet a favor at the same time. The entire set of equipment will cost less than $200. See box on page 128 for ordering information.

LEARN HOW TO HARNESS THE SUN FOR PERSONAL SOLAR POWER TO RECHARGE YOUR CELL PHONE, IPOD, CD PLAYER, AND OTHER DEVICES.

! SAFETY FIRST !

Be sure to have an adult helper with you at all times when you're setting up your power station. During each of the following steps for this activity, check for proper polarity by making sure that the end of each wire is always connected to the same kind: positive to positive (red to red) and negative to negative (black to black). Even when the polarity is correct, it's normal sometimes to see a small spark when connecting two wires, so don't worry. Always use a sealed battery and recycle any battery that is cracked or leaks. Think of the adult as a free source of alternative energy! **Danger of Shock:** Never use your 12-volt power supply anywhere near a bathtub, shower, pond, or any other source or body of water.

WHAT YOU WILL NEED

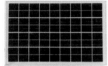

★ Solar photovoltaic (PV) panel

This is a small, 12-volt photovoltaic panel that you place in the sunlight to create electricity. It needs to be big enough to charge your battery with enough power to last several hours when you're drawing power in the evening (minimum solar panel size: 10 watts, 0.6 amp hour).

★ Solar PV charge controller

This little device feeds the unpredictable power received from the Sun by your PV panel and evens it out so that it doesn't harm your battery. It also keeps the battery's power from damaging the solar panel when it is not gathering energy from the Sun. Some PV charge controllers even tell you how much power the solar panel is generating and how charged up the battery is at any time.

★ Connecting wires (wiring harness)

Although the wiring for the Personal Solar Power system is not complicated, it does require a set of specific wires, connectors, and a small fuse, all of which have to fit together just right (see page 128).

★ Tools: small Phillips-head screwdriver or small slot-head screwdriver

★ 12-volt battery (there are many kinds of 12-volt batteries)

A permanently sealed motorcycle battery will work fine for storing the power collected by your solar panel. It's small, costs less than a car battery, won't leak acid, and you won't need to add fluid (minimum capacity: 12 volts, 7 amp hours).

NOTE: *A solar panel is rated for how much electrical power it produces — for example, 10 watts. A battery is rated for amp hours, which tells you how much energy it stores when fully charged.*

★ 5-amp in-line fuse

★ "Cigarette lighter" style, 12-volt "female" outlet

Use this for plugging in any 12-volt device that can be plugged in to an automobile's 12-volt outlet, such as a cell phone, a laptop, or a desk lamp that has been converted to run a 12-volt bulb.

★ 3 small electrical screw-cap connectors

★ 12-Volt Battery Tester

A simple, inexpensive 12-volt battery tester or a digital multi-meter will allow you to measure the power that is both feeding into, and coming out of, the battery for your Personal Solar Power, Mini-Windmill Power (page 160) and Pedal Power (page 192) stations.

DO THE DEED

First, lay out all your materials on a clean, dry surface so you know what you have. Assembling the Personal Solar Power system is not hard if you take your time, focus, and follow directions to make sure you do everything just right.

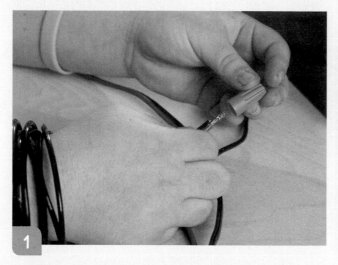

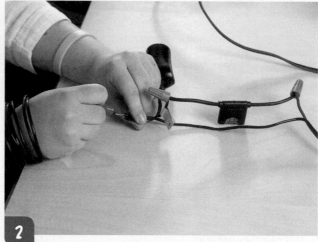

Find the wiring harness that includes the little plugs that are made to slip over the tabs on the battery terminal. (*Don't plug them onto the battery yet.*) Locate the end of the wiring harness on which the bare end of the red (+) wire is shorter than the bare end of the black (–) wire. Use a screw cap connector to attach this red (+) wire to one end of the fuse line.

Use a screw cap to connect the other end of the fuse line to the red (+) wire on the lighter-style plug. Then, use another screw cap to connect the black (–) wire on that same end of the wiring harness to the black (–) wire on the plug.

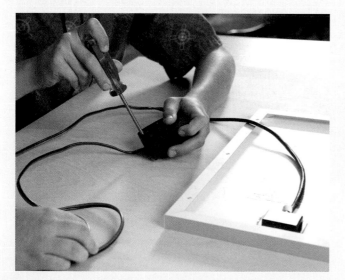

3   With the solar panel lying face down and away from any light so it isn't generating electricity, connect the solar panel wires to the **input** side of the charge controller: red to the positive terminal and black to the negative terminal. Loosen up the screws on the charge controller, slip in the bare end of each wire, and tighten the screw onto the wire firmly.

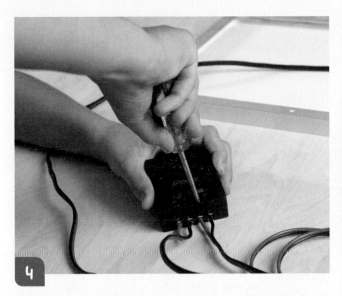

4

Find the end of the wiring harness on which the two bare ends of wire are of the same length. Connect the ends of these wires into the **output** slots on the charge controller: red to the positive terminal and black to the negative terminal, following the same procedure as you did in Step 3.

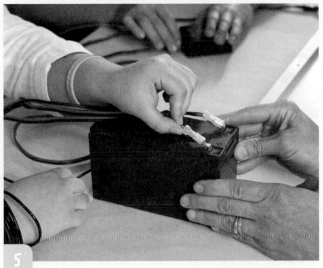

5

Once you've assembled all of the wiring (*and only then*), connect the wiring harness to the battery terminals by slipping the small plugs on the end of each wire over the metal tabs on the battery. Be sure to connect the red wire to the positive terminal on the battery and the black wire to the negative terminal.

6   Place the solar panel in a sunny location facing south and angled slightly up at the sky, so that it will catch the most sunshine.

7   Allow the battery to charge for a sunny day. Now you're ready to plug in any 12-volt-powered device that has a lighter-style plug (the kind that can go into an automobile), such as a cell phone charger, laptop computer charger, or iPod charger. Enjoy the power of the Sun!

YOUR PERSONAL SOLAR POWER SYSTEM ASSEMBLED

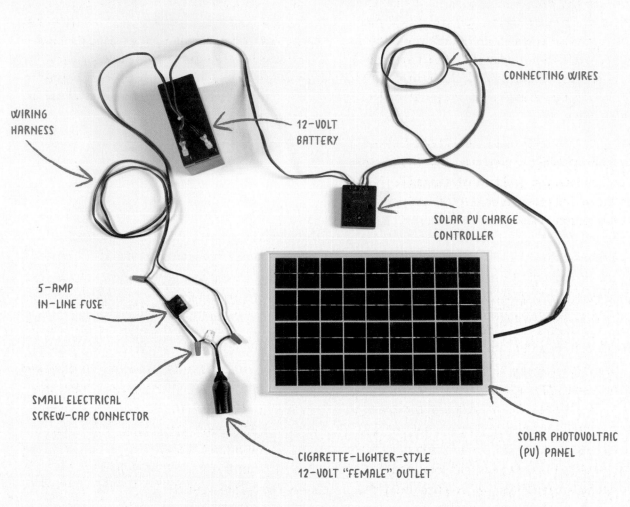

CONNECTING WIRES

WIRING HARNESS

12-VOLT BATTERY

SOLAR PV CHARGE CONTROLLER

5-AMP IN-LINE FUSE

SMALL ELECTRICAL SCREW-CAP CONNECTOR

CIGARETTE-LIGHTER-STYLE 12-VOLT "FEMALE" OUTLET

SOLAR PHOTOVOLTAIC (PV) PANEL

ORDER YOUR SOLAR ENERGY KIT

You can order a complete set of everything you will need for your Personal Solar Power system from Sundance Solar Products, Inc. (See Resources, page 215). Order the **10-Watt Economy Do-it-Yourself Kit.** This setup will capture and store enough solar energy to provide several hours of 12-volt power each day. Sundance Solar also carries a 12-volt DC desk lamp that will run on your PSP System.

⌾ You can find every kind of device, from a small radio to a vacuum cleaner, that will run directly on power that comes from your 12-volt battery. Just search online under "RV 12-volt appliances" or "camping 12-volt appliances." Stores that sell gear for camping and cabins often carry 12-volt electronics.

⌾ Find a small motor that runs on 12-volt power and invent things to be powered by that motor. For example, you could attach a small fan blade to the motor, mount it on a stand, and use it to cool yourself on hot summer days.

⌾ With a little inventiveness you can replace a normal desk-lamp plug with a lighter-style plug, then screw in a 12-volt bulb and plug the lamp directly into your PSP system. **Caution:** *Never screw a 12-volt bulb into a lamp that is plugged into 120-volt household current; this will blow out the bulb.*

LA DC VITA

If you wanted to power an entire house on photovoltaic (PV) electricity, you'd have to spend thousands of dollars installing a group of solar panels, called a *solar array,* and connecting it to your home's AC electrical system. Instead, you can use a single 12-volt personal solar panel to power and charge things that you use every day. Small energy savings add up to a huge amount over time, especially when the savings from hundreds of millions of people are totaled. A 12-volt solar panel can charge the battery to your cell phone, iPod, and computer. Low-energy lights, such as *LEDs* (light-emitting diodes) and the lights you see on people's front lawns, can be powered by 12-volt DC current. These kinds of lights are super efficient. Standard, incandescent lights use only 10 percent of their energy to create light, but LEDs use almost 80 percent of their energy to create light. So not only are LEDs energy efficient, but they're **cool** lights to use, as well.

PART 4

CATCH THE WIND

CHAPTER 12

WHAT DRIVES THE WIND?

"Ah, but I may as well try and catch the wind."

— Donovan, singer/songwriter

What is it about the wind that captures our imagination? Maybe it's the mystery that surrounds something that we can feel but cannot see. The wind can be a gentle breeze brushing our cheek or a powerful cyclone driving a tsunami down upon the shore. It can come as a tornado that lifts a house off its foundation or as the softest puff that causes a frond of fern to wave from the shade of the forest floor.

The wind has inspired many sayings. Something pleasant may be "as refreshing as a summer breeze." A person who is swift afoot is said to "run like the wind," but one who uses too many words is "long-winded." Someone who is being cautious will "wait and see which way the wind blows." And an event or person who is helpful "puts the wind in your sails."

EARTH, WIND, AND FIRE

Energy from the Sun creates the wind. Heat from the Sun warms the air. Heated air rises because it's less dense and weighs less than cooler air. As the warm air rises, cooler, heavier air moves in beneath it. This moving air is what we call **wind.**

As you know, Earth's surface is not flat. It is made up of hills, mountains, and valleys. This affects the direction of the wind and how hard it blows. As wind rides up the slopes of a mountain and is squeezed beneath the high ground and the upper atmosphere, it picks up speed. Air that is forced through the narrow places between city buildings also blows faster. This is called the **venturi effect.**

Habitat also affects the wind. Air rushes across wide-open spaces, like the prairies, where there are no trees or high hills to slow it down. Deserts, forests, and plains change temperature more quickly than lakes and oceans, which affects how the wind forms and moves. Land near the *equator,* the imaginary line that divides Earth into the Northern and Southern hemispheres, receives much more direct sunlight, and solar heat, than areas to the far north and south. Ice and snow in the polar regions and on mountaintops reflect a lot of sunlight and heat, which helps to keep these environments cold.

Also, Earth spins on its *axis,* meaning it spins as if turning around an axle or stick that goes through it from the North to the South Pole. As it spins, Earth's surface moves from west to east. This movement affects how the wind blows. Earth's rotation causes wind to move to the right north of the equator and to the left in the Southern Hemisphere. This is called the *Coriolis effect,* and it's why *hurricanes* (severe tropical storms north of the equator) move counterclockwise and *cyclones* (severe tropical storms south of the equator) move clockwise. It's also why wind generally blows from west to east in North America.

DAILY WIND PATTERNS

Because air over the land heats up and cools down faster than air over the water, the morning Sun first heats up the air along the shore of a lake or ocean. When that air rises, the cooler air over the water moves in beneath it. This forms a *sea breeze* or *lake breeze.* At the end of the day, the air over the land cools down faster than the air over the water. As this cooler air sinks down over the water, it creates a *land breeze.*

A SEA BREEZE

In the morning, warm air over the land rises and cooler air over the water moves in beneath it.

A LAND BREEZE

As night approaches, the air over the land cools more quickly and sinks down over the water, sliding beneath the warmer sea air.

GREEN GIANT

MONARCH WAYSTATION

BENJAMIN WORKINGER, CHATTANOOGA, TENNESSEE

MONARCHS CATCH THE WIND

When Benjamin Workinger was in second grade, he read in the *New York Times* that fewer monarch butterflies were migrating between their northern breeding grounds and their winter habitat — small stands of forest in the mountains of southern Mexico. Trees were being cut in the monarch's winter home, and the milkweed on which they laid their eggs during the summer was becoming less common. Plus, says Benjamin, "Farmers cut down the milkweed because it makes their cows' milk taste sour."

So what was a seven-year-old to do? Benjamin's parents, who he says are "nature nuts," have instilled in him a sense of wonder and concern for protecting the natural world. He just had to take action.

Growing Support for a Habitat

Benjamin approached his classmates and told them what was happening. With permission from the headmaster at Bright School and help from Benjamin's mother, Dr. Catherine Colby, they created a waystation for migrating monarch butterflies. **Waystations** are gardens where the monarchs that are migrating north during the spring and summer can stop to lay their eggs and where autumn migrants heading south can rest and feed on flower nectar. The garden is planted with several species of milkweed on which the adult monarchs can lay their eggs and the larvae (caterpillars) can feed. It is also full of nectar-producing flowers for the adult butterflies to feed upon, including giant coneflower, wild indigo, mammoth dill, and Carolina pea.

Benjamin points out that growing a garden is hard work: "After the garden was planted, we still had to water the plants, weed, and sometimes plant more plants." The effort was well rewarded with an event that Benjamin says is a highlight of his experience: "seeing a monarch come to our completed waystation to lay its eggs. We watched the eggs hatch and the caterpillars become butterflies." Come autumn, these young butterflies continued their migration south.

The garden that Benjamin started is now officially registered in the Monarch Watch Web site database as Monarch Waystation #1857. The people of Monarch Watch, an organization that is based at the University of Kansas (see Resources), helped Benjamin get started by giving him not only tips for planning his garden, but caterpillars as well. "My project is important because the waystation I planted is the breeding ground of

monarchs," says Benjamin. "Butterflies are worth helping because they help pollinate plants." The environmental group Action For Nature recognized the value of Benjamin's extraordinary work with monarch waystations in its 2008 International Young Eco-Hero Awards.

A Call for Gardens

According to Monarch Watch, 1,000 monarch waystations need to be planted every day to replace the monarch habitat that is constantly being lost as land is cleared for development. Fortunately, more than 3,300 waystation gardens are already being grown. Waystations can be created wherever there is a plot of land that can be planted, no matter how large or small, whether along the margin of an old field, in the wild fringe of a city park, or along the edge of a suburban schoolyard.

Benjamin says, "People could make their own waystations for Monarch Watch. They can also plant milkweed and nectar-producing plants, then grow and release monarch caterpillars."

The monarch waystation at Bright School has inspired others, including one that was planted at a local botanical garden, another at a nearby school, and several in the yards of local families.

Benjamin thinks that global warming is the most important environmental issue of our time because it will affect the survival of so many species and habitats. In fact, the growing number of late-summer storms, with their high winds and heavy rains, could have a negative impact on migrating monarch butterflies. Despite these larger concerns, Benjamin continues to work locally and encourages others to do so. "If you like working in gardens," he says, "make a monarch butterfly waystation. This will turn a boring area into a place full of wildlife. Remember: The only

plant that monarchs will lay their eggs on is milkweed, so don't cut it down!

"Even if you're a kid without much knowledge or money, you can do something to help this species and the planet.

BREEZERFLIES

Monarch butterflies from eastern North America overwinter by the millions in areas of only 20 to 30 acres (8–12 hectares) in the mountains of southern Mexico. Their western counterparts migrate south along the coast and roost in eucalyptus trees and Monterey pines between San Francisco and Los Angeles.

The following spring, these butterflies journey north, laying eggs on milkweed along the way. These eggs hatch and produce the next generation, which continues the migration north. Several generations are born during the summer, each of which lives from 6 to 8 weeks.

The special generation of monarchs that hatch in late summer and return to the wintering grounds in the south are the great-great-great-grandchildren of the ones that flew north in the springtime. Some of these late-season monarchs journey over 3,000 miles (4,830 km) and have been seen riding the strong winds at an elevation of 11,000 feet (3,353 m)! During their short, 7- to 8-month life span, they migrate south, overwinter, and fly north again in the springtime to renew the monarch's amazing life cycle.

PIE-PLATE WIND MAKER

In nature, the Sun is the source of heat and of wind. In this activity, the rising warm air created by burning candles turns a windmill.

LEARN HOW WIND IS CREATED WITH THE PIE-PLATE WIND MAKER.

WHAT YOU WILL NEED

* Scissors
* Aluminum pie plate
* Fine-tipped permanent marker
* Ruler
* Small Phillips-head screwdriver
* Small jelly jar or glass with an opening about 2 inches (5 cm) wide
* Pair of cutting pliers to cut the tail off the pen cap
* Pen cap that is pointed at the closed end
* Modeling clay
* Clean, dry, short glass soda bottle with a narrow neck, 8- to 16-ounce size (0.25–0.5 L)
* 3-inch (7.5 cm) sewing needle
* Four tea light candles
* Matches

MAYBE YOU'VE BEEN ASKED THIS OLD RIDDLE:

"If someone on a ship flushes a toilet and the water in the bowl starts to drain clockwise and then the ship crosses the equator, will the water start draining in the opposite direction?" (For the answer, see page 141).

DO THE DEED

Are you ready to manipulate the forces of nature to create wind power?

1

Use scissors to cut the edge from an aluminum pie plate, leaving just the flat center disk. Be careful to not cut yourself on the edge of the aluminum.

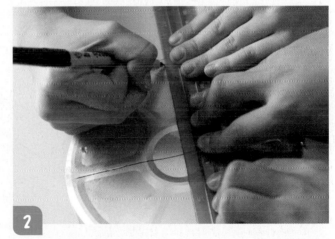

2

Locate the center of the aluminum circle: Place the disk on a table and with the marker and ruler draw one line from the top of the disk to the bottom, passing directly through the center. Draw another line from the left side to the right side, crossing the first line in the center. Your lines will look like the lines of a compass drawn north to south and east to west. The place where the lines cross marks the center of the aluminum disk.

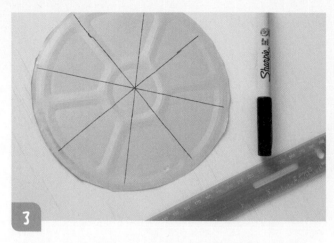

3

You've already drawn two lines that make your aluminum disk look like a pie cut into four pieces. Now you want to make eight equal-size pie wedges, so draw two more lines from one side of the plate to the other, cutting each of the four "pie" pieces in half.

4

Use the Phillips-head screwdriver to poke a small hole through the center of the disk. Using the bottom of a drinking glass or jelly jar as a stencil, trace a circle about 2 inches (5 cm) wide around the center hole while keeping the hole directly in the center of the jar.

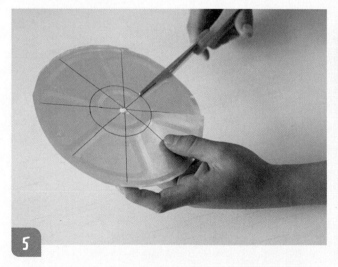

5

With the scissors, cut along all the lines from the edge of the disk up to the outer edge of the circle drawn in the center. (Don't cut into the center circle.)

6

Twist each blade slightly by about 30 degrees so they are all angled in the same direction, like the blades of a windmill or propeller. This will make the disk turn in the rising warm air.

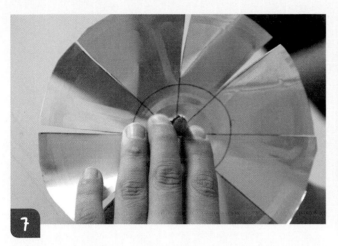

7

Cut the tail off the plastic pen cap with the cutting pliers. Then push the tip of the pen cap through the center hole of the pie plate. Use the screwdriver to expand the hole if necessary. Set this aside.

8

Roll the modeling clay into a ball about the size of a golf ball. Push the ball halfway into the opening in the neck of the soda bottle.

9

Push the thread-hole end of the sewing needle down into the clay about an inch (2.5 cm), leaving the sharp point sticking up. The part of the needle sticking up above the clay must be long enough so that the pen cap will spin freely on the needle without touching the clay along the bottom edges.

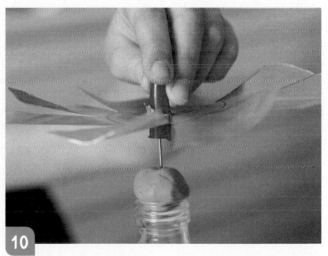

10

Set the open end of the pen cap over the needle. If the pen cap drags in the clay, either raise the needle up a bit higher or use the cutting pliers to cut enough off the bottom of the pen cap so that it spins freely.

11 It's important that the windmill be well balanced. If it is tilting to one side, trim about ⅛ of an inch (3 mm) off two or three blades on the heavy side. Repeat if necessary until the windmill rides evenly on the pen cap.

12 Place the four candles around the base of the soda bottle, evenly spaced, with each wick directly underneath the middle of the windmill blades.

13 Light the candles; the rising warm air will cause the windmill to spin.

THE BIGGER PICTURE

Why does the pie-plate windmill turn? As the air warms, it becomes less dense and weighs less, so it rises. In this activity, the wind is generated by the energy of the burning candles; in nature, the wind is driven by energy from the Sun.

Pilots of hot-air ballons use large gas torches to fill giant bags with hot air. The lightweight hot air rises and carries the balloons up into the sky.

THINK ABOUT IT

- If you live near a lake or pond, go down to the water's edge on a calm, clear morning just before sunrise and float a toy sailboat, or even a leaf, upon the water.  What happens to the sailboat when the Sun rises? Why? Be careful if you do this at the end of the day, however, because the land breeze will blow your boat out toward the open water.

- Hang a lightweight piece of fabric outside by tying it, as high as you can reach, to a fence, to the branch of a tree or shrub — to whatever is available. The next time there's a still, sunny morning, watch the cloth just before sunrise, and continue to check it periodically for about an hour afterward. What happens? Why? Make similar observations during several other calm sunny days and compare the results.

THINK HARDER

- Since colder air is heavier than warmer air, what should happen when you open the door to a refrigerator or freezer? Will you feel the cold breeze by placing your hand in the crack above the door as it opens or in the crack below it? Try doing both to see what happens.

NOW, REALLY THINK

- How could you use a small, toy electric motor and some wire to make this power-plate turbine generate electricity? Design and sketch your own invention.

ANSWER TO RIDDLE ON PAGE 137:

No. If the water has started draining, it will not change direction when the ship crosses the equator. The direction water drains depends more on the shape of the toilet bowl and the direction of flow from the water jets in the toilet. The Coriolis effect (page 133) doesn't tend to affect the movement of such a small amount of water.

PARTY-BALLOON WIND GAUGE

You don't need a complex piece of equipment to figure out where the strongest winds are in your yard.

COMPARE WIND STRENGTH IN DIFFERENT PLACES IN YOUR YARD BY USING THIS PARTY-BALLOON WIND GAUGE. THIS WILL SHOW YOU WHERE TO PUT YOUR WINDMILL!

! SAFETY FIRST !

Stay completely away from electrical power lines and be careful not to let the balloon get close to nearby trees. If your balloon or string touches an electrical line, you can be killed by the electricity no matter what kind of line you use. However, always use cotton or nylon string; never use metal wire or a wet line. Stop immediately if you hear thunder or see lightning.

WHAT YOU WILL NEED

* Tape measure
* Scissors
* Ball of string
* Two helium-inflated party balloons (one to use, one spare in case the first one pops)
* Brick or block of wood
* Pen or pencil
* Pad of paper

DO THE DEED

If you don't have a yard, or if your yard is too small to catch the wind, you can do this same activity at a park, school recreation area, or other similar public space.

1 Measure and cut a 12-foot (3.75 m) piece of string

2 Tie one end of this string to the neck of the balloon and tie the other end of the string onto the brick or small block of wood.

3 Draw a simple map of your yard on the pad of paper.

MAP OF YOUR YARD

Place your Party-Balloon Wind Gauge in several locations to observe where the wind is strongest.

4 Place the brick and balloon in a location in your yard where you think the wind is strongest. Mark that location on your map with a number 1.

5 Watch the angle of the string that holds the balloon to see how strong the wind is. When the wind blows hard on the balloon, the string will tilt at a greater angle and come closer to the ground. After watching the balloon for 5 to 10 minutes, draw a diagram on another page of the pad of paper showing the ground and the angle that the balloon is tilting in that location (see photo above and to the right). Mark diagram with the number 1.

6 Move the balloon to a new location in the yard and mark that location on your map with the number 2. Observe the balloon again at this location, then draw another diagram showing the average angle of the string at location 2.

7 Move the balloon several more times to locations where you think the wind would be strong and repeat the observations and diagrams at each location.

8 When you're done, look at your diagrams and decide at which location the angle of the string is greatest. This is the place where the wind is strongest in your yard. You will want to place your Mini-Windmill Power station, described on page 161, here.

DID YOU KNOW?

Weather forecasters measure the strength and direction of the wind using *wind vanes*, *wind socks* (long, hollow tubes of lightweight fabric), and devices called *anemometers*, which spin faster as the wind blows stronger.

THE BIGGER PICTURE

Here are some other ways that you can measure and observe the wind.

THINK ABOUT IT

⊘ Try letting the balloon out on string that measures 20, 30, and 40 feet (6, 9, and 12 m). At which height do you notice the wind is strongest when observing the balloon?

⊘ If there is a tall tree or rooftop in or near your yard, run up the balloon on a piece of string that is taller than that treetop or rooftop (but far enough way that it doesn't touch). Does the wind blow stronger or lighter when the balloon is raised above the treetop or rooftop? Why does this happen?

THINK HARDER

⊘ Try inventing your own simple wind gauge. For example, you might create a wind gauge based on how fast the wind blows a pinwheel in different locations.

NOW, REALLY THINK

⊘ Use a protractor to measure (on your diagram) the angle between the string and the ground. Which indicates a stronger wind: a larger angle or a smaller one?

Which balloons indicate a stronger wind is blowing: the ones in the photo above, or those in the photo on the opposite page?

CHAPTER 13

WIND POWER

"OF ALL THE FORCES OF NATURE, I SHOULD THINK THE WIND CONTAINS THE LARGEST AMOUNT OF MOTIVE POWER — THAT IS, POWER TO MOVE THINGS."

— Abraham Lincoln, "Discoveries and Inventions"

Why is it important to understand the wind before creating power from it? Because this helps you know whether the place you live has enough steady wind to catch that energy. Here are some good places to live for creating wind power:

- Along the seacoast or shore of a large lake

- On the west-facing slope or top of a hill or a mountain

- On the Great Plains, from Texas to Canada

- Along a narrow pass between hills or mountains, which often funnels the wind

- In a windy space between tall buildings in a city

- Wherever the wind is steady and has an average speed of 9 miles (14.5 km) per hour or greater

FORECAST: A CHANCE OF WIND, POTENTIAL FOR ENERGY

The U.S. Department of Energy has created maps that show where, in each state, the wind is best for creating power. Visit the website (see Resources) and click on your state map. Then click on the place where you live on your state map until it becomes larger.

Environment Canada has posted the Canadian Wind Energy Atlas online (see Resources). Click on the map location near where you live, then add your postal code to focus on the map for your location.

FIVE THOUSAND YEARS OF SAILS

Wind power has been around for thousands of years. The first sailing craft were ancient dugout log canoes fitted with animal-skin sails. More than 5,000 years ago, Egyptian sailboats skimmed across the waves while powered by wind pushing cloth sails.

When you think of windmills, you may picture four-sail, low-to-the-ground Dutch windmills — the kind seen nestled among the tulips in folklore and fairy tales. But the earliest windmills were built in Persia (now Iran) nearly 1,400 years ago. Eventually, the Dutch invented windmills with blades covered by cloth sails, arranged like giant pinwheels. By the twelfth century, more than 10,000 windmills turned in the winds that blew across western Europe — grinding grain and pumping water.

Although we tend to think that generating electricity from the wind is a new technology, the first electrical generating windmill was built at a Danish high school by a physicist named Poul la Cour in 1891!

Egyptians have sailed the seas for more than 5,000 years.

GUESS WITH GUSTO

What . . .

... *is almost always moving but goes nowhere?*

... *is rooted in the ground but isn't alive?*

... *works by the Sun's heat but not by its light?*

... *has blades that cut nothing but air?*

... *is found on a farm but doesn't grow?*

For the answer to this riddle, see page 153.

Two of Poul la Cour's wind turbine prototypes at Askov Folk High School, Denmark, 1897.

SAIL AWAY

Sailboats are one of the oldest ways ever invented for putting wind to work.

LEARN THE BASIC PRINCIPLES OF SAILBOATS BY MAKING THIS MINIATURE CRAFT, AND LET IT CAPTURE YOUR IMAGINATION AS IT SAILS ACROSS THE WATER.

! SAFETY FIRST !

Use the handsaw, the drill, and the knife under adult supervision. Always be careful when playing in and around water. Even shallow water can be dangerous if you fall in and hurt yourself. Be sure you have an adult with you when you go to sail the boat for this activity. Don't ever stand up in a canoe or rowboat, and always remember to wear a life preserver when out on the water.

WHAT YOU WILL NEED

* Pencil
* Ruler
* 12-inch (30 cm) wooden dowel of ½-inch (13 mm) diameter
* Carving knife
* Handsaw
* Waterproof glue
* Cloth from an old sheet or shirt; it should measure at least 12 inches (30 cm) square
* Scissors
* 3 clothespins
* Piece of white pine or other lightweight wood measuring 4 inches (10 cm) wide by 8 inches (20 cm) long and ¾ inch (2 cm) thick
* Sandpaper (medium grit, #80)
* Drill and ½-inch (13 mm) drill bit
* Tape
* A pond or other body of water

OPTIONAL

* A few metal washers or coins
* Small figures or animals

DO THE DEED

Take the following steps to make a simple boat, and have some fun catching the wind.

1 Use the pencil and ruler to make a mark 4 inches (10 cm) up from one end of the dowel. This is where you will eventually cut the shorter *cross-piece* or *spar* off the main mast.

2 Now make another mark 2 inches (5 cm) up from that same end of the dowel. This is where you will carve the notch that helps the spar to fit onto the main mast. (It is much easier to carve this notch while the spar is still attached and you have a long piece of dowel to hold on to.)

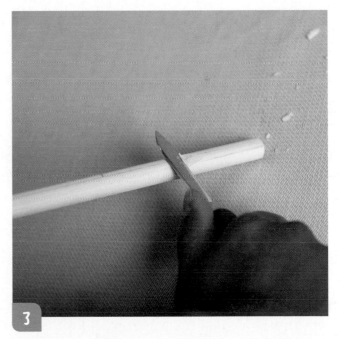

3 With the carving knife, carefully carve a shallow U-shaped notch at the 2-inch mark. The notch has to be only deep enough to fit together with the longer piece at a 90-degree angle.

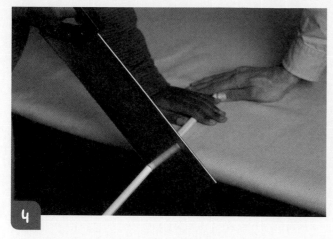

4

With the handsaw, cut the dowelling into two pieces: The smaller notched piece should measure 4 inches (10 cm) and the larger piece should measure 8 inches (20 cm). The longer piece will be the mast; the shorter piece, the spar.

5

Glue the notch in the short piece onto the long piece, about 2 inches (5 cm) from one end. Let the glue dry thoroughly.

6

Lay the mast assembly on top of the piece of cloth. Draw the triangle shape for the sail by connecting the three points formed by the top of the mast and two ends of the spar. Trace an extra ½-inch (1.25 cm) of width all around the entire edge of the triangle.

7

Cut the cloth along the edges of the triangle that include the extra ½ inch.

8 Wrap the upper tip of the sail over the mast and glue it in place. Hold this together with a clothespin while the glue dries. Fold and glue the bottom edge of the sail along the spar. Fasten a clothespin on each end to hold the sail in place until the glue sets.

9 Spread a thin bead of glue along the remaining, exposed edges of the sail and fold over that extra ½ inch to make a seam so the cloth doesn't unravel. Set aside this sail assembly to dry.

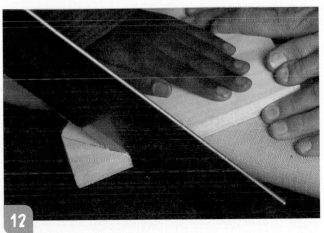

Using the ruler and pencil, mark the center on one end of the 8-inch- (20 cm) long piece of wood. This point will be the bow of the sailboat.

11 Now mark the wood on each side about 2 inches (5 cm) back from that end. Draw lines connecting the bow point to each of the marks on each side. This will create a point shaped like an arrow.

Use the saw to cut along each of the lines to create a point on the front of the board. Your sailboat is taking shape.

13

Sand the edges of the sailboat until they are smooth.

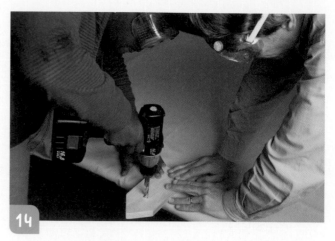

14

Make a mark about 3 inches from the point of the bow and in the center of the board. Carefully drill a hole about ½ inch (1.25 cm) down into the board at this point. This is where you will attach the bottom of the mast.

15

Once the sail assembly is dry, place a dollop of glue into the hole.

16

Very carefully, pick up the sail assembly and, holding the main mast only, insert the mast into the hole and lightly twist back and forth until it works its way down into the hole. Be careful not to touch the spar piece along the bottom of the sail or it could break off. Make sure the front of the sail faces the bow on the front of the sailboat. Wipe away the excess glue from the bottom of the mast. Let this glue dry completely.

17 Before you take your boat out for a sail, float it in a sink or tub and make sure it is floating level. If not, tape a few metal washers or coins onto the top of the lightweight end until the weight has evened out and the boat is floating flat in the water.

18 Take your sailboat to a pond or marsh — a small body of water that you can walk all the way around — on the next breezy day.

19 Set your sailboat into the water on the upwind (windward) side of the pond. Watch it sail across, then catch it on the downwind (leeward) shore. If you want, attach a few small figures of people or animals onto the deck of the boat and watch them sail across the water.

◎ Ask around until you find a friend or family member who has a sailboat or knows a good friend who has a sailboat. Tell that person you're studying the wind, and ask if he or she would be kind enough to take you out for a ride on a sailboat and teach you something about sailing. Be sure to wear a life vest.

◎ If you have a rowboat or canoe, you can rig a simple sail. Lash together two oars or paddles into the shape of a mast and spar, and use a sheet or blanket to make a sail by tying the corners into place with twine or light rope. Hold this sail toward the front of the boat, with someone in back to balance your weight, and catch the wind. Do this while sitting or kneeling in the boat (with your life vest on); don't stand up or you could easily tip over the boat or fall in.

◎ Use your imagination and create a more realistic, detailed version of your first Catch the Wind sailboat. You'll soon find that making and sailing beautiful model sailboats is a popular hobby and that people are passionate about their boats.

◎ Imagine being aboard your own sailboat as it glides across the pond. Write about the adventures you have while sailing, such as riding out a bad storm or meeting other sailors or the animals that live in and around the pond or ocean.

◎ Read "A Fair Breeze" and "The Sailboat Race" in *Stuart Little* by E. B. White.

? GUESS WITH GUSTO

If you guessed **"a windmill"** as the answer to the riddle on page 147 . . . you're right!

Learn more about windmills and wind turbines in the next chapter.

CHAPTER 14

WINGED TOWERS

"To every Thing . . . Turn, Turn, Turn
There is a season . . . Turn, Turn, Turn"

— Pete Seeger, folksinger and songwriter

Modern windmills catch the energy of the wind's movement and turn it into a circular motion that powers a *generator* (turbine) to produce electrical energy.

Blades on most of today's wind turbines are shaped like the wings of an airplane: one edge is wider than the other and one surface is curved outward. When the wind rushes over the wider, curved side it spreads out, forming an area of low pressure on that side of the blade and higher pressure on the other side. This creates a force called *lift* that causes the blade to turn toward that low pressure.

Some of today's turbines are as tall as a 20-story building. The larger blades are more than 200 feet (60 m) long. This means that the big circular area that is swept by these blades is over 400 feet (122 m) across: **longer than a soccer field.** This is called the *swept area* of a

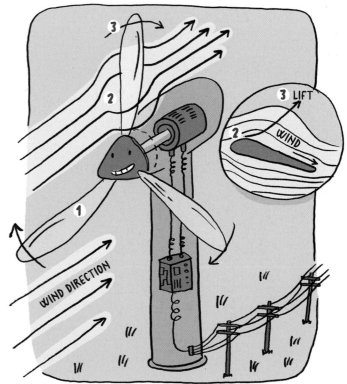

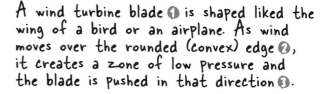

A wind turbine blade ❶ is shaped liked the wing of a bird or an airplane. As wind moves over the rounded (convex) edge ❷, it creates a zone of low pressure and the blade is pushed in that direction ❸.

wind turbine (picture the circle created by the spinning propeller on an airplane).

Another kind of electrical generating wind turbine that is not as common looks like a giant eggbeater pointed at the sky. This wind tower is often only about 100 feet (30 m) high and 50 feet (15 m) wide.

One large wind turbine generates up to 5 megawatts (5 million watts) of electricity when turning. If we built enough wind generators, we could create seven times the electricity required to supply the needs of the entire world. In 2008, the United States was creating enough electricity from wind to meet the needs of 4.6 million of its 106 million households.

ONE LARGE WIND TURBINE GENERATES UP TO 5 MEGAWATTS OF ELECTRICITY

Large numbers of electrical generating wind turbines built close together are often called a **wind farm.** The Horse Hollow Wind Energy Center in Texas is the largest wind farm in the United States. It has 421 turbines that can power **220,000 homes.** Iowa, Minnesota, and Oklahoma are other leading wind-power states. But California produces twice as much electricity from wind power as any other state: enough to light up a city as big as San Francisco, with plenty to spare.

A row of wind turbines in Searsburg, Vermont.

The vertical-axis wind turbine resembles a giant eggbeater. Blades use the force of lift to create motion and can spin faster than the speed of the wind driving the turbine.

HOW WIDE THE WINDMILL'S WHIRL?

Here's how you can calculate the swept area — the size of the circle created by the whirling blades of a fan or windmill:

> **The magic formula: $pi \times r^2$**
> **pi = 3.1415 and r = radius**

1. First, figure out your radius. The radius is equal to the length of the blade, so if you have a windmill with a blade that measures 200 feet (60 m) long from the center of the windmill to the end of the blade, then that blade's length is the radius.

2. Next, square the radius and multiply it by *pi*. (radius × radius) × *pi*

For example:

$(200 \times 200) \times 3.1415 = 125,660$ square feet

Since 1 acre = 43,560 square feet, 125,660 square feet ÷ 43,560 = 2.9 acres

So a windmill with blades that are 200 feet long sweeps around a circle of airspace that is about 3 acres in size!

In meters:

r^2 (60 m × 60 m) = 3,600 square meters × 3.1415 = 11,309 square meters

Since 1 hectare = 10,000 square meters, 11,309 square meters ÷ 10,000 = 1.1 hectares

A windmill with blades that are 60 meters long sweeps around a circle of airspace that is about 1.1 hectares in size!

WIND POWER BLOWS HOT AND COLD

Catching the wind can be an Earth-friendly way to generate electricity. It is a method that lacks the negative effects of burning coal, oil, and natural gas or using nuclear fuel in electrical power plants.

But large wind farms have to be planned very carefully or they, too, can seriously impact the environment. Wind turbines are often built in beautiful remote natural areas, such as deserts, mountaintops, and shallow oceans. This construction, plus the presence of large wind turbines, can disturb the scenery and fragment the habitats of plants and animals. Power lines that carry electricity from wind turbines to the electrical grid have to be cleared through natural habitat, and those power lines are strung on poles that often pass close to, or even through, people's property.

Migrating birds are not attuned to the unnatural threat posed by wind turbines which need to be located away from flyways or birds can be maimed and killed in the swept areas of the turning blades. Although many people think windmills are beautiful, many others prefer to see an unspoiled hilltop or prairie, rather than a wind farm. And the turning blades make a whooshing or whining sound that disturbs people who live close by.

PARTS IS PARTS: THE 125-YEAR WINDMILL DESIGN

Today's wind turbines range from small home designs that are barely taller than a person to wind towers that are far bigger and more complex than the thousands of wooden windmills that pumped water from the ground to supply farms all across the Great Plains in the late 19th century. But the basic parts of a windmill haven't changed that much. Each windmill has (see illustration at right for location):

❶ **a footing** to hold the tower in the ground

❷ **a tower** to support the blades

❸ **a rotor** that turns like an axle at the center of the blades

❹ **blades** attached to the rotor that cause it to spin when the wind blows

❺ **a tail or rudder** that directs the rotor into the wind, or some other kind of device that accomplishes the same task

❻ **a turbine** that generates electricity as the rotor turns

SSTB — SAVE SMALL AND THINK BIG

Even when your electricity comes from wind power, it pays to use less energy so you don't have to generate as much. We gain big time when we *SSTB* — **Save Small and Think Big** — because every little bit of energy saved adds up to a great deal over time. The cheapest and most Earth-friendly form of energy is the energy we don't use. Think about it.

Parts of a wind turbine (see text at left)

MAJOR MILL-AGE

More and more homes and businesses are putting up small- and medium-size wind turbines to create their own electricity. Most are of the pinwheel design, some are the upside-down eggbeater type, and still others look like blades of sails turning in the wind. Then there's the silent, sculpturelike Energy Ball (below), which can generate as much as half of a home's electrical needs and measures just 6.5 feet (2 m) across. (See Resources.)

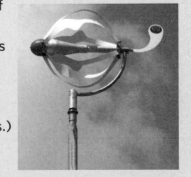

GREEN GIANT

NATHAN MOOS, SANDY, UTAH

NO IDLING

GREEN GIANTS

IDLE-FREE GIRLS, STONEWALL, MANITOBA (LEFT TO RIGHT): DESTINY GULEWICH, NEELY SWANSON, KATELYN MORRAN, AND RACHEL PERRELLA

CLEAN AIR, HEALTHY PEOPLE

Idle minds, they are not. What does Nathan Moos of Sandy, Utah, have in common with Neely Swanson, Destiny Gulewich, Katelyn Morran, and Rachel Perrella, all of Manitoba — a quartet of environmental activists who call themselves the Idle Free Girls? If you answered that they all like to laze about the house, you couldn't be more wrong. These students share a passion for clean air.

Ponder this: Exhaust from a car that idles (sits with its engine on) for 5 minutes each day can, in one year, create 30 pounds (14 kg) of toxic pollution and 300 pounds (140 kg) of carbon dioxide that add to global warming. These fumes also contain tiny particles that lodge deep inside the lungs. Because kids are smaller and take more breaths than adults, they inhale 50 percent

more pollution for each pound of body weight. Exhaust gases cause serious problems for youth with asthma, and asthma is the leading cause of hospital visits for children.

Idle-Free Teenagers

A few years ago, in the Canadian town of Stonewall, Manitoba, four ten- and eleven-year olds decided they'd breathed enough. These fifth-graders, spurred into action by Al Gore's documentary An Inconvenient Truth, expanded an "Idle-Free Zones" program at the Stonewall Centennial School. Neely, Destiny, Katelyn, and Rachel became the "Idle Free Girls."

"We wanted to take that campaign to the next level," they said, "so we made our first presentation to our Town Council as fifth-graders.

They were very supportive of our ideas, and now we have dozens of Idle-Free Zone signs all over town.

"We educate and encourage schools and towns to create idle-free zones in school parking lots, parks, streets, and sporting areas. We educate individuals about why they should turn off their engines if they will be idling for more than 10 seconds, and the harmful effects of idling."

The Idle Free Girls have had lots of help and support from their teacher, Mrs. Kari Kinley, who organizes bookings, helps them prepare presentations, and drives them to their destinations. "Our parents all support our project by not letting their cars idle," say the Girls. "The Climate Change Connection gave us brochures to give people, and Manitoba's minister of Science, Technology, Energy, and Mines had business cards printed for us."

The Idle Free Girls have won many accolades, including a Gold Award at the Y.E.S. (Youth Encouraging Sustainability) Showcase and the 2008 Manitoba Eco-Network Environmental Group Award. They've been featured in newspapers and magazines, and have appeared on environmental websites, TV, and even CBC Radio. Now, practically celebrities, the Idle Free Girls have met with the premiers of Manitoba and British Columbia, the governor of Arizona, and the CEO of the Climate Group in the United Kingdom.

No Idle Campaign

About 900 miles south and west of Stonewall, Manitoba, in the hot, dry climate of Sandy, Utah, lives Nathan Moos. Here, in the Salt Lake Valley, schoolchildren breathe some of the most polluted air in the United States.

One day, when he was eleven, Nathan noticed his mother turn off her engine while waiting in a drive-through line in order to cut down on pollution. Inspired with an idea, he organized classmates to hand out educational flyers and demonstrate with signs asking bus drivers and parents to turn off their engines whenever they were waiting on school grounds.

On the first day, the buses arrived soon after Nathan and his friends lined up and held up their signs. "I thought that if we showed teamwork, it would help. When the drivers saw all of the signs, they started turning off the engines: 63 times in a row!" Nathan exclaims.

Empowered by success, Nathan pushed on, talking to his school principal and proposing a schoolwide ban on idling. Then he took a huge step and promoted his cause before the Utah state legislature's Transportation Committee, asking them to pass an anti-idling bill.

"Now," says Nathan, "there is a program supported primarily by Salt Lake County called 'Idle Free Utah.' It has a huge support base but best of all, it aims to prevent idling in elementary schools. They have all sorts of information about car idling, especially if in Utah."

In 2008 Nathan received an International Young Eco-Hero Award from Action For Nature. He offers this advice: "Think before you act. This is an important thing in all aspects of life. I learned that myself. Think whether your actions will have any sort of environmental consequence. Try to do things in the most ecofriendly way as possible."

JOIN THE GREEN SCENE

If you want to start your own Idle-Free campaign, you can do it much easier than you may imagine. Idle-Free Zone signs are available on the Web (see Resources).

MINI-WINDMILL POWER

This is a fairly simple plan for making a small windmill at home. It can help to charge a 12-volt battery for use when charging your cell phone, iPod, laptop, or other 12-volt electronic device.

PRODUCING **MINI-WINDMILL POWER** IS A CREATIVE, FUN FAMILY EXPERIENCE THAT HELPS YOU LEARN HOW THIS KIND OF SYSTEM WORKS.

! SAFETY FIRST !

Always have adult supervision.
Monitor the windmill created in this activity to make sure it is working properly and is being used safely. **Put up the tower only when you plan to use it, and store it carefully when it's not in use.**

Do not risk getting hit by lightning. Check weather forecasts before putting up and using your Mini-Windmill Power station. *Lower the tower all the way down at the first forecast of a thunderstorm, before the bad weather begins!* If you can hear thunder, it's already too late to safely take down the tower because lightning leaders can strike in advance of an approaching storm. Go indoors until the danger has passed completely. If thunder and lightning come up suddenly, do not go outside and risk getting hit by lightning just to retrieve the windmill.

Even if strong winds alone are predicted, you should protect the blades and turbine of your windmill from being damaged. Untape each joint of the pole and telescope it down, one section at a time. Then slip the windmill assembly off the top and store it in a safe place until the wind has passed.

Danger of Shock: Never use your 12-volt power supply anywhere near a bathtub, shower, pond, or any other source or body of water.

WHAT YOU WILL NEED FOR THE MINI-WINDMILL STAND

* Tape measure
* Permanent marker
* 1 piece of 5-foot-long (1.5 m) PVC wire conduit pipe, 1¼ inches (3.2 cm) in diameter (you'll need to purchase this as a 6-foot length and cut off 12 inches)
* Safety goggles
* Hacksaw
* 1 piece of medium-grit (#80) sandpaper
* Heavy metal mallet
* One 4-foot- (1.2 m) long wooden surveyor's stake, 1 inch (2.5 cm) square, and sharpened to a point on the end
* Level

* Duct tape
* One 15-foot (4.5 m) aluminum telescoping golf-ball retriever
* Tin snips

Optional (for staking your Mini-Windmill stand in high-wind areas)

* 24-foot (7 m) length of strong clothesline rope
* Pair of scissors
* 3 sturdy tent stakes

DO THE DEED

Before deciding on where to place your completed Mini-Windmill Power station outdoors, use the activity called Party-Balloon Wind Gauge, on page 142, to find the location in your yard where the wind is strongest.

This Mini-Windmill works well in winds of 5 to 15 miles (8–4 km) per hour. When spinning freely, it generates about 50 watts of power that will slowly "trickle-charge" the 12-volt battery that is also part of the Personal Solar Power station (page 124) and the Pedal Power station (page 192).

PART I: MAKING THE MINI-WINDMILL STAND

You'll need an adult helper for this activity.

1 Use the tape measure and the marker to mark off a 5-foot (1.5 m) length of the PVC wire conduit pipe.

2 Put on your safety goggles, then cut off the excess piece of conduit pipe with the hacksaw.

3 Rub the freshly cut edge of the pipe with the sandpaper to remove any rough edges.

4 Use the mallet to drive the pointed end of the wooden surveyor's stake into the ground at the location where you've decided the wind is strongest in your yard or on the school grounds. Drive it down a few inches at a time and recheck it with the level on both sides to make sure it is straight. Keep hammering the stake a few inches and rechecking with the level until the end of the stake is buried 16 inches (40 cm) or so into the ground and is standing straight. If the soil is loose, you may need to drive the stake a bit deeper to make sure it's securely anchored and won't wobble or blow over.

5 Place the piece of conduit pipe up against the wooden stake, with the end that you cut against the ground. Use the level to make sure it, too, is standing straight up.

6 Use the duct tape to fasten the conduit pipe securely to the wooden stake. Place three tight wrappings of duct tape around the stake and pipe: one near the top of the stake, one near the bottom of the stake, and one in the middle.

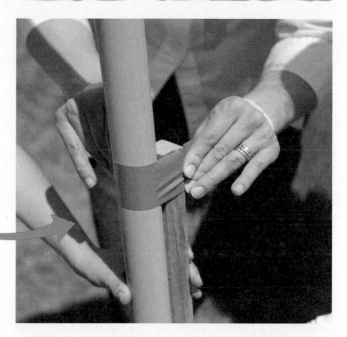

Use the hacksaw to cut off the bracket on the end of the golf-ball retriever, so that the only thing left is the end of the upper tube. Rub the sandpaper over the rough edges to remove any burrs from the cut end of the tube.

Extend the bottom segment of the golf ball retriever and tape that joint, then slide the bottom (handle) end of the golf ball retriever into the hole in the PVC pipe. If the handle wobbles, use a few wrappings of duct tape to secure it in the center of the pipe so that the golf ball retriever is standing up straight.

If you live in an area of moderate to high winds, continue with steps 9–12 to stake your Mini-Windmill stand and make it stronger.

9 Use the scissors to cut the piece of clothesline into three pieces, each 8 feet (2.5 m) long.

10 Tie the ends of all three pieces of clothesline to the Mini-Windmill stand, just above where the aluminum support comes out of the top of the PVC pipe.

11 Evenly space the ropes around the windmill stand and stake to the ground. Make sure the tension in the ropes is equal all around the windmill so that it stands up straight and is not being pulled off to one side.

SPECIAL DESIGN FOR PLACES WITH LIGHT WIND

Some readers may require a Mini-Windmill with a rotor and tail assembly created especially for use in places where the wind speed is slow much of the time. This design uses six blades and a longer tail and tail fin that will keep the blades spinning in light winds. For a materials list and step-by-step assembly instructions, see Appendix.

WHAT YOU WILL NEED FOR THE MINI-WINDMILL

Note: The parts with an asterisk (*) come with the Mini-Windmill Kit recommended for this activity (see Resources for kit-ordering information). You will need to obtain other parts and tools separately.

The following generator unit comes preassembled.

✳ One 50-watt geared generator*

✳ One 1-inch- (2.5 cm) long threaded arbor, matching machine bolt, and jam nut for attaching the plastic disk that will hold the windmill blades to the generator (the arbor comes attached to the generator)*

✳ 1 T-shaped metal bracket on which the generator is mounted (¾ inch [2 cm] in diameter × 13 inches [33 cm] long, with a 5-inch [13-cm] shaft)*

✳ Two 5-inch- (13 cm) long pieces of steel band attaching the generator to the T-shaped bracket*

✳ 2 machine bolts measuring 1½ inches (4 cm) long × ¼ inch (0.6 cm) wide, with 4 matching flat washers and 2 matching nuts (these bolts will hold the generator to the T-shaped bracket)*

Additional parts and tools needed to assemble the Mini-Windmill:

✳ 10 flat ("fender") washers for the ¼-inch- (0.6 cm) diameter machine bolts*

✳ One 5-inch- (13 cm) diameter, round plastic disk/hub made of 3/16-inch (0.5 cm) ABS plastic with holes drilled for attaching 3 windmill blades*

✳ 2 adjustable wrenches

✳ 6 machine bolts measuring 1 inch (2.5 cm) long × ¼ inch (0.6 cm) wide*

✳ Three 17-inch- (43 cm) long PVC windmill blades with holes drilled for bolting to the plastic disk*

✳ 8 matching ¼-inch (0.6 cm) nuts for the machine bolts*

✳ 2 machine bolts measuring 1½ inches (4 cm) long × ¼ inch (0.6 cm) wide*

✳ One 8-inch × 9-inch (20 cm × 23 cm) angled tail fin*

✳ 1 tube-shaped plastic generator cover*

✳ Allen wrenches (hex key wrenches)

✳ 30 feet (9 m) of 14-gauge two-strand wire insulated for use outdoors — the kind in which one strand of wire is red and the other is black

✳ Cutting pliers

✳ Needle-nose pliers

✳ Roll of electrical tape

✳ Wire stripper

✳ Scissors

✳ Roll of duct tape

✳ Small Phillips-head or slot-head screwdriver

✳ 12-volt battery tester (optional)

Parts needed to power a light directly from the Mini-Windmill:

✳ Bicycle light

✳ Electrical tape

✳ Phillips-head screwdriver

✳ Adjustable wrench

PART II: ASSEMBLING AND WIRING THE MINI-WINDMILL

1   Unthread the bolt from inside the arbor (it already has a "jam" nut attached). Slip a washer onto that bolt, below the nut.

2   Insert the threaded end of the bolt/washer/nut assembly through the hole in the center of the round plastic disk/hub.

3   Slip another washer onto the end of the bolt once it's sticking through the hub.

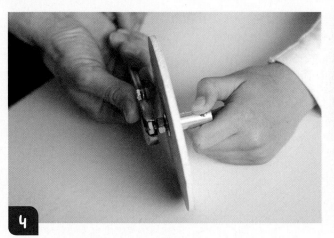

4

Now thread the bolt back into the hole in the arbor.

5

Hold the arbor steady with the needle-nose pliers while using an adjustable wrench to tighten the bolt clockwise, until it just touches the bottom and seats snugly in place.

6   Continue to hold the arbor with the needle-nose pliers while using the adjustable wrench to tighten the jam nut. This will secure the plastic disk/hub onto the end of the arbor.

7

Use six of the 1-inch (2.5 cm) machine bolts to attach the three windmill blades to the round plastic hub (two bolts for each blade; blades and hub come with holes already drilled). Place the flat surface on the wide end of each blade up against the round hub, so the inside of the curve will face the wind. Slip the bolts in from the front side of the blades and through the round plastic hub. Attach a flat washer and nut onto the threaded end of each bolt and use the wrenches to tighten firmly but not too tight.

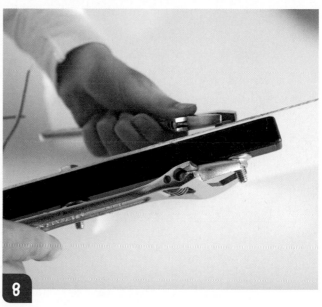

8

Use two of the 1.5-inch- (4 cm) long machine bolts, flat washers, and matching nuts to attach the tail fin to the rear of the bracket that holds the motor. Tighten the bolts snugly using the adjustable wrenches.

9

Slide the plastic cover over the motor.

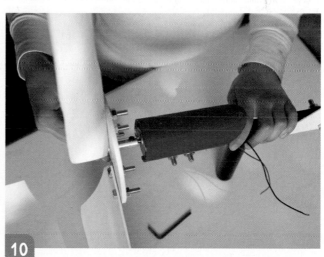

10

Attach the windmill-blade assembly onto the generator by sliding the hole in the arbor over the end of the generator shaft. Tighten the Allen (hex) screw in the arbor using an Allen wrench.

11 On one end of the 30-foot (9 m) length of wire, use wire strippers to expose a 1-inch (2.5 cm) piece of bare wire on the ends of both wires. Do this by gently closing the mouth of the wire strippers an inch below the end of each wire and carefully pulling off the coating. Do the same thing to expose the two wires on the other end.

12 Using the long wire and the needle-nose pliers, twist one end of the red strand of wire onto the positive (red) wire coming from the generator. Wrap this tightly with electrical tape.

13 Twist the black wire onto the exposed end of the negative (black) wire coming from the generator. Wrap with a piece of electrical tape.

14 Take the completed mini-windmill assembly outdoors. Place the open end of the T-shaped mounting bracket onto the end of the golf-ball retriever that is standing up in the Mini-Windmill stand. Slip the windmill down over the top one or two telescoping segments, until it reaches the segment that is just the right thickness to hold the windmill while still allowing it to swivel freely.

15 Extend the telescoping section of the golf-ball retriever (the segment that is just below the windmill assembly) to its full length, then wrap a piece of duct tape around the lower joint to hold it securely in place.

Pull up on the next telescoping section until it's fully extended. Tighten the joint and wrap a piece of duct tape securely around the bottom of the joint from which that section extends.

    Keep extending and taping the bottom of each section until your windmill is about 10 feet (3 m) off the ground. Be sure to keep the wire loose as you extend the pole for the windmill. Now gently wind the wire around the pole a few times so it doesn't flap in the wind.

Create a wide loop of loose wire at the base of the windmill and tape it off at the bottom of the loop with electrical tape. This will allow the windmill to turn in the wind without causing the wire to bind.

Hook up the ends of the wire leading from the wind tower to the input slots on the charge controller that's attached to your 12-volt battery (see Personal Solar Power on page 128). Attach the red wire to the positive slot and the black wire to the negative slot.

    Tighten the screws on the charge controller firmly to hold the ends of these two wires in place. Now, whenever the blades are turning at a moderate speed, the wind power will charge your personal renewable energy source.

NOTE: The DC generator will only create a positive charge when turning in one direction. If the wind is turning your windmill quickly but the light on the charge controller is not coming on, then the generator may be turning in the wrong direction and is not charging the battery. (A reading taken with a 12-volt battery tester would display a negative voltage.)

In this case (only), switch the wires running from the windmill into the charge controller so that they are hooked up opposite to how they would normally be connected: fasten the red wire into the negative terminal and the black wire into the positive terminal.

19 As an alternative, you could use the long piece of 14-gauge wire as an extension to hook up a bicycle light or any other light that runs on 6-volt-to-12-volt power. Link the wire that comes directly out of the bicycle light to the red wire from the Mini-Windmill generator. Wrap those connections with electrical tape. Now link the black wire coming from the generator to the bolt on the metal bracket that the bicycle light is mounted on. Flip the switch, and you have a wind-powered light.

Wind is a kind of energy that's all around us most of the time, even though we can't see it. When we catch the wind to make electricity, we take one kind of energy and turn it into another kind of energy. Windmills enable us to use the wind's energy to generate the power that we need in everyday life.

THINK ABOUT IT

By watching your Mini-Windmill as it spins and swivels, you can see how the wind is behaving. Which direction does the windmill face most of the time? What does this tell you about the direction the wind is blowing from? Why do you think the wind comes mostly from that direction?

THINK HARDER

When you use your Mini-Windmill, you are working with two major kinds of energy:

Kinetic energy is the energy of something in motion.

Potential energy is energy that is stored, like that in a watch spring.

What kind of energy is found in the wind? In the moving parts of the windmill? In the electricity created by a windmill? In the battery that stores the power created by the windmill?

MAKE IT BIGGER

If you want to use the knowledge and skills you gain from your Mini-Windmill Power experience to create a larger homemade wind turbine, websites with step-by-step instructions can be found in Resources.

NOW, REALLY THINK

- The first electrical generating windmills were used in Denmark in 1891. So why do North Americans still create such a small amount of electrical power from the wind today, compared to the amounts of electricity we create from other kinds of energy?

- If you could choose, where and how would you get all your electricity?

- Can you think of any location that is very close to power lines and where there are poles on which to attach small-scale windmills?

PART 5

CRANK UP THE POWER

CHAPTER 15

ALL CHARGED UP

"To electrise plus or minus, no more needs to be known than this, that the parts of the tube or sphere that are rubb'd, do, in the instant of friction, attract the electrical fire, and therefore... are disposed to give the fire they have received, to any body that has less."

— Benjamin Franklin

A woman living in ancient Greece is getting dressed up for a formal visit with some friends. She chooses her favorite jewelry: a piece of amber that has been carved into a pendant the shape of the Sun. As she places the pendant around her neck, she notices that it's smudged. She rubs the amber against her dress, hears a slight crackling sound, and finds that some strands of her hair have stuck to the amber. She lifts up the pendant, and her hair rises with it.

The ancient Greeks were the first to write about observing this natural event. In this imagined scene, when the woman rubbed the amber onto her dress, the amber picked up electrons from the fabric and the extra

The ancient Greeks got a charge out of static electricity.

electrons created a charge on the surface of the amber. The woman's hair was then attracted to that charge, so it stuck to the amber. That charge is called **static electricity**.

When it comes to electrical forces, opposite charges **attract** (pull toward each other) and similar charges **repel** (push away from each other). Rub a balloon against your hair, and the balloon picks up extra electrons and therefore takes on a **negative charge**. Hold the balloon against a wall, and it will stick because it is more negatively charged than is the wall.

WHEN IT COMES TO ELECTRICAL FORCES, OPPOSITE CHARGES ATTRACT AND SIMILAR CHARGES REPEL.

Your hair, meanwhile, has lost electrons, so it now has a **positive charge**. Since the strands of hair have the same charge, they repel. That's why static electricity makes your hair become frizzy and stand on end. Each piece of hair is trying to get away from the others!

We think of static electricity as the shock we get when we shuffle across a rug on a dry day and then touch a doorknob, some other metal surface, or even another person. As our feet move along the carpet, we pick up electrons and literally become charged up.

A balloon gathers electrons (−) when you rub it against your hair. That negative charge creates an attraction to protons (+) in the wall and causes the balloon to stick.

Then, when we touch something that is in contact with the ground that the charge can flow into, our **extra electrons fly off our body** at that point of contact, creating a painful spark.

Simply pulling a sweater off in the dark when the air is dry generates enough static electricity to create shocks that we can hear as crackling sounds and sparks that we see as pinpoints or squiggly lines of light. These charges are generated as electrons separate from the atoms they're orbiting around.

BALLOON JOKE

Two balloons were hanging around, just stuck to a wall. One balloon fell off the wall, looked up at the other, and said, "Some people just rub me the wrong way."

STATIC BALLOONS & BAD HAIR

Think about why the balloons and your hair behave the way they do when trying Static Balloons & Bad Hair.

BALLOONS ARE SO LIGHTWEIGHT THAT THEY REACT TO VERY SMALL FORCES THAT PULL OR PUSH AT THEM, SO THEY ALLOW US TO SEE HOW

NEGATIVELY AND POSITIVELY CHARGED OBJECTS

RESPOND TO EACH OTHER.

WHAT YOU WILL NEED

* Two round balloons
* String
* Scissors
* Mirror
* Hair
* Different surfaces

DO THE DEED

1 Blow up the balloons and knot the ends or tie them off with string.

2 Rub all sides of a balloon against your hair for about 30 seconds. Only the parts you rub will become charged.

3 Place the balloon against a wall, then let go of it.

4 Rub the other balloon against the hair on the other side of your head.

5 Stick this balloon onto a different kind of surface, such as against wooden paneling or onto the metal side of a refrigerator.

6 Now look into a mirror to see what your hair is doing.

THE BIGGER PICTURE

Who would think that electrons — atomic particles that we can't even see — could have such a major impact on our everyday lives? The strongest forces in nature are often invisible, and there's the rub.

THINK ABOUT IT

⊘ What happened after you rubbed the balloon against your hair and then placed it against the wall and let go? Do you know why? (If not, search this chapter for the answer.)

⊘ What was happening to your hair when you looked in the mirror? Why was it behaving that way?

⊘ Do some other low-energy activity, then come back and see which balloon has fallen down first. Why do you think one balloon fell off one kind of surface before the other balloon fell off the other kind of surface?

⊘ Why does your hair stand up when you pull a sweater up over your head?

⊘ Tie a piece of string onto the neck of each of the two round balloons and hang them from an object overhead so that they are dangling evenly and the sides are barely touching. Rub both balloons against your hair and charge them up. Are they attracted to or repelled from each other? Now, very slowly, move one of your hands toward a balloon. Watch how the balloon reacts as your hand comes closer. Why do you think the balloon does this?

CHAPTER 16

ELECTRO-MAGNETISM

"The Force will be with you, always."

— Obi-Wan Kenobi

Lightning is nature's magnificent electrical show. The motion of rain, wind, and water vapor inside intense storm clouds causes charges to separate: the tops of the clouds become positively charged and the bottoms become negatively charged. At the same time, electrons are repelled on the ground causing tall objects — such as mountaintops, steeples, and trees — to become positively charged. When these charges grow large enough, a violent electrical discharge occurs as a **bolt of lightning — a powerful jolt** of up to 1 billion volts. The thunder that follows is the sound of air rapidly heated from this huge spark.

It's no surprise that Benjamin Franklin saw a connection between lightning and electrical energy. According to legend, in

Lightning jumps from the negative charge at the bottom of a storm cloud to the positive charges of tall objects on the ground, within the same cloud, or in other clouds.

June of 1752, Franklin flew a kite into a thunderstorm with a metal key attached to the string in order to draw sparks. (Since Franklin knew lightning strikes were deadly, he wouldn't have held the string directly in his hand!) Franklin proved his point, but harnessing electricity from lightning was not practical. It was the discovery of the connection between magnetism and electricity, and inventions such as the electromagnetic generator and the battery, that made it possible to produce and store electricity for everyday use.

MAGNETIC ATTRACTION AND REPULSION

Two thousand years ago, people in China believed that a certain kind of rock could be used to predict the future. They named this rock the *lodestone;* we now know it as a mineral called *magnetite.* What familiar word can you find in the name of this mineral?

Every *magnet* has two *poles*: the ends where the magnetic force is strongest. One pole is positive and the other is negative. Oppositely charged poles stick together and similarly charged poles push apart. These poles are surrounded by a magnetic *force field*.

OPPOSITELY CHARGED POLES STICK TOGETHER AND SIMILARLY CHARGED POLES PUSH APART.

THE FIRST BATTERY

In 1800 an Italian named Alessandro Volta found that if plates that are made from two different kinds of metal are connected with something moist, electrons will flow from one plate to the other. The strength of this pull on electrons to flow is called *electrical potential.*

Volta later learned that electrons could flow along a length of wire. In his honor, we now measure the strength of an electrical potential in *volts.* The electrical current itself is measured in *amperes,* or *amps.* When measuring direct current (DC), which is produced by batteries, the amount of *power* (in *watts*) equals volts × amps.

In the electrical device that was created by Volta — the voltaic pile — a small current passed between metal disks made of zinc and copper that were separated by cloth saturated with salt water. This was the first battery ever invented.

Volta's battery worked on the same principle as the "Two Potato Clock" (pictured here). This clock also uses electrical contacts made of zinc and copper to create an electrical potential. In place of cloth soaked in saltwater, the metal contacts are stuck into potatoes or another vegetable or fruit, such as cucumbers, apples, oranges, bananas, or tomatoes. The voltage is strong enough to power a digital clock.

MAGNETIC
ATTRACTION—OR NOT

Once you've tried Magnetic Attraction — or Not, think of a way you can harness the power.

THESE SIMPLE EXPERIMENTS SHOW MAGNETISM IN ACTION BY REVEALING HOW IT AFFECTS THE WORLD AROUND US.

WHAT YOU WILL NEED

* 2 simple bar magnets

* Piece of thin cardboard

* Small jar of iron filings (see Resources)

* Bowl of sand

DO THE DEED

The saying goes that "opposites attract." Regardless of whether this is true for different personalities, it's definitely true for the opposite poles of magnets. But when you try to push the similar poles of a magnet together, they repel.

1 Lay one of the two bar magnets flat on a level table or other smooth surface, with the ends of the magnet facing to your right and left.

2 Hold the other magnet flat against the table but a few feet from the first magnet.

3 Very slowly, bring one end of the second magnet up toward the first magnet. When the second magnet comes close enough to the first magnet (the distance will depend on the strength of the magnets), it will start to react. If similar poles are facing each other at the point of contact, the first magnet will spin around and away from the end of the second magnet. If opposite poles are facing each other, the first magnet will quickly slide over and stick to the magnet in your hand.

4 Now take the piece of cardboard in hand and hold it level.

5 Place one magnet on top and in the center of the cardboard.

6 While holding the cardboard with the magnet balanced on top in one hand, take the second magnet and move it around under the cardboard. Watch how the magnet on top reacts.

7 Now place one magnet on a table.

8 Sprinkle a teaspoon of iron filings onto the cardboard and tap the cardboard to spread it out evenly.

9 Carefully place the cardboard on top of the magnet, with the magnet centered beneath the iron filings.

10 Gently tap the edge of the cardboard, then watch how the iron filings arrange themselves along the magnetic lines.

11 Pick up the cardboard and move the magnet around under the iron filings. How do the iron filings react? Do they react differently at the different poles of the magnet? Why or why not?

12 Hold the magnet and swish one end around in the bowl of sand for a minute or two. When you lift up the end of the magnet, it will have some dark flecks stuck to it. Do these look familiar?

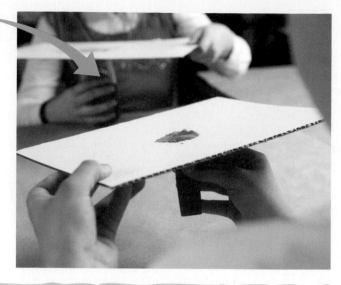

THE BIGGER PICTURE

There seems to be no end to the experiments you can conduct with magnets. Try some of the ones that are described below, and then design some original activities. Once you start toying with magnets, it's hard to stop because they're so much fun. That must be the attraction.

THINK ABOUT IT

⊘ What do you think the magnet picked up in the sand? If you guess a kind of metal, you are right. Iron is a very common metal, and flecks can be found in the soil all around us.

THINK HARDER

⊘ Using two magnets, cardboard, and iron filings, try putting both magnets under the cardboard and moving them around to various positions (as in Step 3 on page 181). Watch how the iron filings form designs as the two magnetic fields interact. Can you use a magnet to separate the iron filings into two piles?

NOW, REALLY THINK

⊘ Think of different ways that you can use the forces of magnetic pull and repulsion to make some simple machines. For example, if you wanted to stir something, you could attach a small magnet to a tiny motor and make this spin underneath a cup holding another magnet. When the magnet beneath the cup spins, it will also make the magnet inside spin — stirring the ingredients in the cup.

⊘ Sketch your simple machine design on a piece of scrap paper.

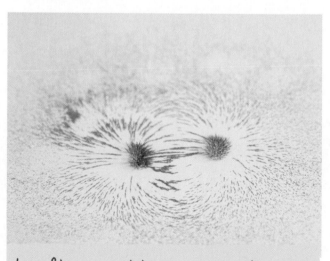

Iron filings reveal lines in a magnetic force field.

CURRENT EVENTS

In 1831 an English engineer named Michael Faraday was experimenting with magnetism when he discovered something that changed the world. He found that when a magnet is moved inside a coil of copper wire, electrons begin to flow through the wire, creating a current. Except for solar power and hydrogen fuel cells (see Resources), virtually every kind of electrical generating system that has been designed since that time is based on Faraday's basic design for a generator.

Today's turbines are modeled after designs invented by two Scotsmen: James Watt (1784) and William J. M. Rankine, who perfected the first steam turbine in 1859. Watts are now used to measure the power of electricity; they are equal to volts times amperes (see page 179).

So magnetism and electrical current are closely related. Not only does a coil of wire spinning near a magnet create an electrical current, but also a magnetic field forms around an electrical current. This electrical magnetism, or *electromagnetism,* is what makes it possible to create television pictures, store data on computer hard drives, and power up electrical speakers, such as those in your stereo, TV, and headphones.

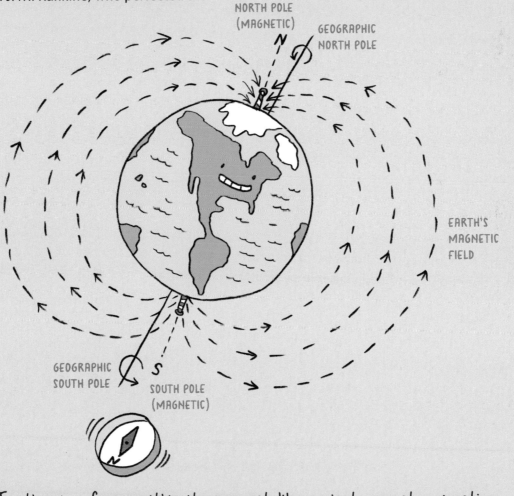

NORTH POLE (MAGNETIC)

GEOGRAPHIC NORTH POLE

EARTH'S MAGNETIC FIELD

GEOGRAPHIC SOUTH POLE

SOUTH POLE (MAGNETIC)

As Earth spins, forces within its core act like a giant generator, creating an electrical current that is the source of its magnetic field.

UN-TRUE NORTH

A compass needle moves so that it lines up with Earth's magnetic field. If brought close to a magnetic field that is stronger in that location, the compass needle will turn and align with that magnetism.

YOU WILL EXPERIENCE A FORCE OF NATURE YOU CANNOT SEE WHEN TRYING UN-TRUE NORTH.

WHAT YOU WILL NEED:

* Piece of thin, bare copper wire about 12 inches (30 cm) long
* 1 size-C battery
* Electrical tape
* Compass
* Small bar magnet

! SAFETY FIRST !

If you are using a new battery, the copper wire and the battery can become very warm. Don't hold the wire in direct contact with your skin for too long, and don't keep both ends of the wire connected to the battery for more than a few minutes.

DO THE DEED

Here is a simple way to detect the magnetic field created by an electrical current.

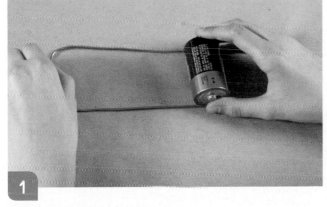

1 Take the piece of wire and bend it into a U-shape, with the mouth of the U matching the length of the C battery.

2 Use a 2-inch (5 cm) piece of electrical tape to fasten one end of the copper wire firmly against the flat side (negative terminal) of the battery. Now tape the other end of the wire onto the small nub sticking out of the other side of the battery (positive terminal).

3 Hold the compass and notice the position of the needle as it points north.

4 Hold the compass about 12 inches (30cm) above the wire, and then move the battery so the wire is parallel to the compass needle.

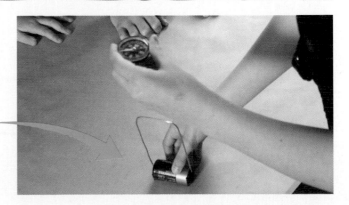

5 Gradually bring the compass close to the wire until it is almost touching. Watch the compass needle turn as it reacts to the magnetic field that surrounds the electrical current running through the wire.

6 Raise the compass again. Now turn the battery 180 degrees so that the ends are switched around. This will reverse the direction the current is flowing around the wire loop.

7 Lower the compass toward the wire through which the current is now flowing in the opposite direction from the first time you did this. When the compass needle turns this time, how is it turning differently from the way it turned in Step 5?

8 Untape the connection on one end of the battery and watch to see if the compass needle changes direction and points back toward the North Pole.

9 Take the small bar magnet in one hand and bring the compass down over it until they are almost touching. How does the compass needle react? Remember which way the North arrow is pointing.

10 Take the magnet away from the compass needle and turn the magnet 180 degrees so that the poles are switched around.

11 Bring the compass toward the magnet again and see which way the North arrow points this time.

THE BIGGER PICTURE

You can "see" magnetism in action by watching it move the compass needle. But what do these things really tell us about magnetism?

THINK ABOUT IT

⊘ Why does the compass needle react as you bring it close to the electrical current flowing through the wire?

⊘ When you disconnect the wire from the battery, does it affect the direction of the compass needle? Why does it do so, or why not?

⊘ Did the compass needle change direction when you flipped over the battery and held it near the wire conducting current from the other end of the battery? How did it react? Why do you think it reacted this way?

THINK HARDER

⊘ After the wire has been hooked up to both ends of the battery for a few minutes, it becomes warm. Why does this happen? Can you think of any household devices that use electricity to create heat?

NOW, REALLY THINK

⊘ When you were using the bar magnet and compass, why did the north end of the compass needle switch directions when you flipped the magnet around and reversed the location of the poles?

⊘ In the real world, strong electrical fields are used to create powerful electromagnets that go on and off when a switch is flipped. Have you ever seen electromagnets being used? Can you think of any uses for electromagnets?

CHAPTER 17

OF GENERATORS AND MOTORS

"I am busy just now on Electro-Magnetism and think I have got hold of a good thing."

— Michael Faraday, 1837

When coils of wire spin inside a set of magnets, or when magnets spin inside coils of wire, this generates an electrical current that passes through the wires, and we call it a *generator*. This principle is used to produce much of the power we use today. Most large generators, called *turbines,* are turned using energy from flowing water (hydropower); or from steam created in power plants fueled by coal, oil, natural gas, or nuclear reactions.

Why is this important? Because we can also use tidal and wind power, plus solar-heated steam, to turn a generator and make electricity from these immense forces of nature. **That's what cranking up the power is all about.**

What would happen if, instead of turning a generator to make electricity, we fed electricity into the generator? You

Parts of a DC motor. Power from the battery ❶ runs through the rotor ❷ to create a magnetic field. The magnetic forces in the rotor interact with the poles of the surrounding magnet ❸ (attracting and repelling) very quickly, which causes the motor to turn. Other parts: brushes ❹, commutator ❺, axle ❻.

already know that when electrical current is fed through wires it creates magnetism. So if we run power into a generator, the coil of wire in the center would become a powerful *electromagnet*.

After experimenting with magnets and balloons, you also know that opposite charges attract each other and matching charges push away from each other. The poles of this powerful electromagnet would react to the poles of the permanent magnets that surround it, causing similar charges to repel and opposite charges to attract. These attractions and repulsions — the actions of the magnets drawn together and pushed apart — happen so quickly that they cause the coil of wire in the center to spin. And that's what we call a *motor.* So a motor is simply a generator with power running into it. If it's a DC motor, it will turn in different directions, depending on how the two wires are hooked up to the connections on the motor.

A more sophisticated motor/generator: Power supply ①, axle ②, rotor (armature) ③, magnets ④.

REEL MATH

In case you ever questioned whether math is relevant to real life, young Eco-Hero Adeline Suwana's basic calculation for the microhydroelectric station proves math matters (see page 190).

She says, "The **power** that we get from the 18-meter **head** of the waterfall combined with the 14.16 liters per second **flow** [volume] of the waterfall comes to 2,500 watts."

➡ **HERE'S THE FORMULA SHE USES:**

Head × Flow × Gravity = Power
18 × 14.16 × 9.81* = 2,500 watts

Now let your math teacher know you never should have doubted her!

*The acceleration due to gravity = 9.81 meters per second

PLAYPUMP

Water is scarce in the dry regions of Africa. Many villagers have to travel far to get water in jugs and carry those heavy loads back home. What can be done?

A group called Roundabout Outdoor has invented a water pump that is hooked up to a merry-go-round. As kids spin the merry-go-round, they also turn a water pump underground. The pump pushes well water up to a 660-gallon (2,500 L) tank overhead. Gravity then feeds the water through a pipe to where it is needed. Many schools have installed PlayPumps for their water supply.

Roundabout Water Solutions built PlayPumps in Lesotho, Malawi, Mozambique, South Africa, Zambia, and Swaziland. This group has already built more than 2,000 PlayPumps. This creative solution to drought may inspire you to invent your own sort of waterwheel! (See Resources for where to find PlayPumps.)

DOING A GOOD TURN.
At 16 spins per minute, PlayPump kids can produce 370 gallons (1,400 liters) of water in an hour.

GREEN GIANT

ADELINE TIFFANIE SUWANA, KELAPA GADING PERMAI, INDONESIA

FRIEND OF NATURE

Adeline was eleven years old and had just graduated from Primary 6 in Indonesia when she first got involved with protecting the environment. "I think the most important environmental issue that we face in Indonesia and the world today is climate change, which has already disrupted our environment and communities," she says.

Many of Indonesia's low-lying coastal farms would flood if sea levels continue to rise due to global warming. Two thousand of the nation's smaller islands could be underwater by 2030. Rising temperatures may shorten the rainy season and make storms more severe. These changes would affect Indonesia's rice yield — the staple food for more than 230 million people.

"Nature is declining in quality at an alarming rate," Adeline says, "starting from where we live and stretching to the sea — the river, the forest, and the air that we breathe. The effects can be felt in the form of floods, air pollution, and beach erosion due to climate change and global warming."

But Adeline is hopeful. Speaking with wisdom beyond her years, she says that starting at an early age, children need to be encouraged to grow a sense of love and caring toward nature and the environment.

Planting Trees in a Fragile Land

How does an eleven-year-old start to save the world? In July 2008, after graduating from primary school, Adeline spent her holiday teaching friends about the importance of mangrove trees. Soon they were planting mangroves at Taman Wisata Alam Angke Kapuk, the Jakarta Mangrove Rehabilitation Center.

She says that in order for the project to succeed, it was important "to make children include their parents so that they start realizing it is time that we contribute to the world to save our mother nature from destruction."

Adeline's enthusiasm is contagious. She and her colleagues soon formed a group called Sahabat Alam, or "Friends of Nature." The number of children who joined Sahabat Alam and the environmental projects they took on grew quickly. The group's activities have included ecotourism, planting coral reefs, freeing Penyu Sisik (hawksbill turtles), and cleaning marine debris from beaches.

Adeline says she feels honored that she was awarded first place in the 2009 International Young Eco-Hero Awards (for ages eight to thirteen) by the San Francisco–based Action For Nature. She was also selected as an Indonesian delegate by UNEP (United Nations Environment Programme) to participate in the 2009 TUNZA International Children's Conference in Daejon, Korea, in August 2009.

Adeline doesn't see herself as being much different from any other twelve-year-old. "I am not the only Eco-Hero," she says. "Children, youths, and adults all over the world can do the same thing as long as they have the willingness and commitment. This comes first from the heart, then from sharing with friends and starting to take action."

Helping Rural Families

Adeline also sees the connection between the needs of people and the natural world: "I would like to help our remote brothers and sisters to fulfill their dream [of] flowing electricity into their houses for children to study, watch television, cook, and all other activities, especially at night." Nearly half of Indonesia's 235 million people live without electricity.

The solution? An Electric Generator Water Reel, a small hydroelectric generator that uses the natural power of a waterfall to produce what Adeline describes as "clean, environmentally friendly, Green, renewable, and sustainable energy that does not increase the amount of carbon dioxide in the atmosphere or worsen the greenhouse effect." The water reel simply turns in the falling water and doesn't affect the waterfall or the flow of the stream. (See Reel Math on page 188.)

Thanks to help from parents and sisters, and, more recently, the Indonesian Ministry of Environment, Sahabat Alam brought power to the village of Kampung Cilulumpang, in the region of South Cianjur, West Java, which is a 4-hour drive from Jakarta. The group is now building Electric Generator Water Reels for two other villages, and it plans to bring this project to villagers throughout Indonesia.

"Previously, children's voices were not heard," says Adeline, "but now we are coming together to voice our commitment to our national leaders and world leaders, to make peace and start having one voice to save the Earth.

"We are the next and future generations of the world. In our hands, the world and its contents are at stake."

> "IT IS **TIME THAT WE CONTRIBUTE** TO THE WORLD TO **SAVE** OUR MOTHER **NATURE** FROM **DESTRUCTION.**"

Sahabat Alam, "Friends of Nature" (See website in Resources)

PEDAL POWER

If the Sun isn't shining
and the wind won't blow,
then you can saddle up and
make some pedal power flow.

THE **PEDAL POWER** STATION SHARES THE SAME ELECTRICAL COMPONENTS AS THE PERSONAL SOLAR POWER DESCRIBED IN CHAPTER 11 AND THE MINI–WINDMILL POWER IN CHAPTER 14, EXCEPT THAT IT USES A BICYCLE–POWERED GENERATOR. (SEE PHOTO ON PAGE 128.)

! SAFETY FIRST !

Always have adult supervision when working with electrical current, gears, and other moving parts. (Adults are also a great source of pedal power!)
Keep fingers, clothing, and wires away from the bicycle chain, sprockets, and spokes.

Danger of Shock: *Never use your 12-volt power supply anywhere near a bathtub, shower, pond or any other source or body of water.*

WHAT YOU WILL NEED

* **20-inch (50 cm) bicycle**
(This can be an old bike, and if you don't have access to a 20-inch bike, a similarly sized one will do.)

* **Bicycle training (fitness) stand**

* **12-volt DC generator (motor), measuring roughly 2.5 inches (6 cm) long × 1.5 inches (4 cm) in diameter (see Resources)**

* **One 1-inch- (2.5 cm) long metal arbor with a ¼-inch (about 6 mm) threaded hole and Allen (hex) tightening screw for attaching the training wheel onto the generator shaft (see Resources)**

* **Allen wrenches (hex key wrenches)**

* **1 machine bolt (¼-inch [6 mm] diameter thread × 1.25 inches [3.2 cm] long)**

* **1 flat metal washer (¼-inch hole [6 mm] and ¾-inch [2 cm] diameter)**

* **5-inch (13-cm) bicycle training wheel (with rubber tire)**

* **Needle-nose pliers**

* **Adjustable wrench (medium sized)**

* **1 standard frame-mounted, bottle-shaped bicycle-light generator (see Resources)**

* **2-inch (5 cm) hose clamp**

* **Slot-head screwdriver (medium sized)**

* **2 Phillips-head screwdrivers (medium sized and small)**

* **10 feet (3m) of 14-gauge, two-strand wire insulated** for use outdoors (the kind in which one strand of wire is red and the other is black)

* **Wire stripper**

* **Cutting pliers**

* **5 electrical screw-cap line connectors**

* **Charge controller**
This little device feeds the variable power received from the bicycle generator and evens it out so that it doesn't harm your battery (an overcharged battery can explode). It also keeps the battery's power from damaging the generator when it is not in motion.

* **12-volt, deep-cycle, sealed battery**
There are many different kinds of 12-volt batteries. A **sealed** battery that won't leak acid and is the size of a motorcycle battery will work fine for storing the power collected from your Pedal Power Station. (Minimum capacity: 12 volts, 7 amp hours.)

* **5-amp, in-line fuse**

* **Cigarette lighter-style, 12-volt "female" outlet**
Use this for plugging in any 12-volt device that can be plugged in to an automobile's 12-volt outlet, such as a cell phone, a laptop, a desk lamp that has been converted to run a 12-volt bulb.

* **12-volt battery tester (optional)**

DO THE DEED

Creating power with the Pedal Power station is not about hopping aboard and pedaling as fast as you can to keep a lightbulb lit. This power station does the same thing that the Personal Solar Power and Mini-Windmill Power stations do: it trickle-charges your 12-volt battery so you can draw power when you need it. Here's how to set up your Pedal Power station (PPS):

1 Mount the rear wheel of your bicycle in the bicycle training stand and clamp it down firmly.

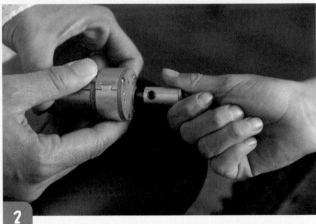

2 Fit the arbor over the end of the shaft on the 12-volt generator. Tighten the arbor by using an Allen wrench of the correct size — one that fits snugly into the hole and will not slip when you apply pressure to turn the Allen (hex) screw.

3 Slip the flat metal washer over the ¼-inch machine bolt, then slide the bolt and washer through the hole in the center of the bicycle training wheel.

4 Screw the bolt into the threaded hole in the center of the metal arbor and hand-tighten. Be careful to keep the wheel centered on the arbor so it will spin without wobbling.

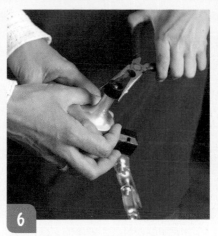

5

Tighten the bolt into the arbor by holding the shaft of the arbor with the needle-nosed pliers while turning the head of the bolt clockwise with the adjustable wrench. Make the bolt snug enough so that the wheel is fastened securely to the generator shaft, but not too tight.

6

Use the adjustable wrench to remove the small bolt from the end of the bottle-shaped bicycle-light generator. Use the needle-nosed pliers to pull off the small ribbed piece that is meant to rub against the tire. (You are only going to use this generator as a bracket onto which you will mount the 12-volt generator.)

7

Slip the hose clamp over the wires on the 12-volt generator and over the generator itself.

8

Place the 12-volt-generator assembly and hose clamp over the narrow end of the shaft on the bottle-shaped bicycle-light generator so that the training wheel will be on the side facing the rim of the bicycle wheel.

9

Use the slot-head screwdriver to tighten the screw on the hose clamp so that it's firm but not too tight. **Caution:** If you tighten the bolt too much, it will squeeze the generator, which will cause the shaft to bind and be difficult to turn. This could damage the gears in the motor.

10

11

Using the mounting bracket and medium-sized Phillips-head screwdriver, mount the bicycle-generator assembly onto the frame on the left-hand side of the bicycle (the side on which your left foot pedals). Slide the mounting bracket along the frame until the training wheel is lined up so that it rides against the sidewall of the tire.

Turn the mounting bracket on the bicycle frame so that the training wheel tilts toward the tire. There should be enough tension that the spring in the mounting bracket holds the training wheel firmly against the sidewall of the tire. If the training wheel slips when the bicycle tire is rotated, increase the tension. When the tension is just right, use an adjustable wrench to firmly tighten the bolts on the mounting bracket.

12

Use the 14-gauge wire to hook up the generator to the charge controller that leads to your 12-volt PPS. First, expose about a half-inch (1 cm) length of bare wire on all six ends of wires: the two ends coming from the generator and both strands of wire on both ends of the length of 14-gauge wire. Do this by gently closing the mouth of the wire stripper an inch below the end of each wire and carefully pulling off the coating.

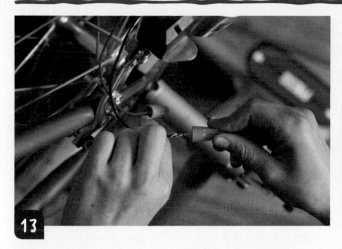

13

14

Match up the end of the red (positive) wire from the bicycle generator to the red end on the 14-gauge wire. Slip an electrical screw cap over these two ends and turn it clockwise until snug. Use the same procedure, and another screw cap, to attach the black (negative) wire coming from the generator to the black end of the 14-gauge wire.

Attach the other end of the 14-gauge wire to the input terminals on the charge controller. Insert the red wire into the positive (red) terminal of the charge controller. Use the small Phillips head screwdriver to tighten the screw of the terminal until the wire is held firmly in place. Follow the same procedure to fasten the black end of the 14-gauge wire into the negative (black) terminal on the charge controller.

15 Find the end of the wiring harness where the red and black wires are the same length. Attach these wires to the output terminals on the charge controller, inserting the red wire into the positive (+) terminal and the black wire into the negative (–) terminal. Tighten the screws firmly. (See schematic on page 128 for tips.)

16 Locate the end of the wiring harness on which the red (+) wire is shorter than the black (–) wire. Use one of the screw-cap connectors to attach a bare wire on the end of the fuse line to the red (+) wire on the wiring harness.

17 Use a screw cap to connect the other end of the fuse line to the positive (+) wire on the lighter-style plug.

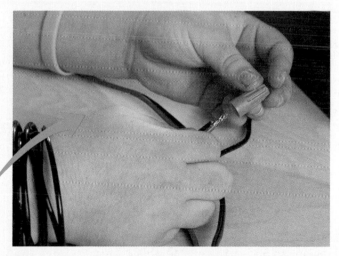

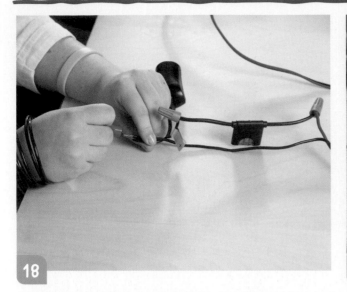

18

19

Use another screw cap to connect the black (–) wire on that same end of the wiring harness to the negative (–) wire on the lighter-style plug.

Finally, connect the assembled Pedal Power System wiring to the battery terminals by slipping the small plugs on the end of each wire over the metal tabs on the battery. Be sure to connect the red wire to the positive terminal on the battery and to connect the black wire to the negative terminal.

NOTE: The DC generator will create a positive charge only when turning in one direction. If you are pedaling steadily but the light on the charge controller is not coming on, then the generator may be turning in the wrong direction and is not charging the battery. (A reading taken with a 12-volt battery tester would display a negative charge.) **In this case (only),** switch the wires running from the bicycle generator into the charge controller so that they are hooked up opposite to how they would normally be connected: Fasten the red wire into the negative terminal and the black wire into the positive terminal.

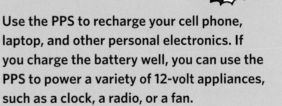

JOIN THE GREEN SCENE

Use the PPS to recharge your cell phone, laptop, and other personal electronics. If you charge the battery well, you can use the PPS to power a variety of 12-volt appliances, such as a clock, a radio, or a fan.

20 Pedal the bicycle and you will see that the light on the charge controller comes on, which shows that current is flowing to the battery. Pedal for several hours, taking turns with friends or family members, or splitting up your time, in order to pace yourself and charge the battery. You can use a medium or high gear, but pedal only at a slow-to-moderate pace. **Don't pedal fast or it will cause the generator to spin too quickly and could damage the gears inside.**

21 Now it's time to use your Pedal Power station by plugging in your iPod, cell-phone charger, laptop — any device that has a lighter-style 12-volt plug — into the matching outlet coming from your battery.

Now you're on the road to grid-free power.

THINK ABOUT IT

◎ Use the battery of your PPS to charge your iPod. Then listen to music while you pedal to create electricity. Save energy and be entertained while keeping yourself in good physical condition.

◎ Hook up a small, 12-volt cooling fan to your PPS and position it so that it blows on your face to keep you cool while you pedal.

THINK HARDER

◎ Set up a small table on which to place a low-energy, 12-volt reading lamp (CFL or LED) that is plugged in to your PPS. Read a book while you pedal. When you become engrossed in a good story, you'll forget you're even pedaling.

◎ Start a PPS Club in your neighborhood and school. Use a network of these Wheel Deals to draw less power from the electrical grid.

NOW, REALLY THINK

◎ Are there other ways you and your friends could use your body to make electricity? Think of repetitive physical activities that you enjoy and which might lend themselves to making power. How could you use those activities to make energy that could be captured for your use? Sketch your invention on a piece of scrap paper.

A ROCK-AND-ROLL RIDE

Turn, turn, turn — get those electrons moving. Personal power stations help you discover the potential of the possible. If you want some inspiration, learn about a rock band called the Ginger Ninjas. This awesome musical group travels to its concerts by bicycle and powers up the shows with pedal power. Check out its website (see Resources).

➡ GO ONLINE TO CHECK OUT THE GINGER NINJAS, A BAND THAT TRAVELS TO CONCERTS BY BICYCLE.

CHAPTER 18

SEEING THE LIGHT

Lightbulbs were among the very first things powered by electrical generators when power was brought into homes and businesses. The change from candles and oil lamps to electrical lighting created a revolution in how active people could be after sunset. Of all the inventions ever created, electrical lighting is simply . . . the most brilliant.

The first electrical lighting was created in 1878 when a British scientist named Joseph Wilson Swan invented the basic **incandescent lightbulb**, which has been the most common kind of lighting used in homes ever since. Incandescent lightbulbs are compact, familiar, and reliable sources of light, but they're also little energy hogs. About 90 percent of the energy used by an incandescent lightbulb turns into heat, so only 10 percent shows up as light.

Incandescent lightbulbs may be small and familiar, but they are big energy hogs!

INCANDESCENT   CFL   LED

LIGHTBULB DESIGNS THROUGH TIME.
Incandescent bulbs date back to 1878 and are the least energy
efficient; LEDs are the newest and most energy efficient.

Fortunately, in the early twenty-first century, two energy-efficient forms of home lighting became available. One is called the compact fluorescent light (**CFL**). These are tiny, screw-in versions of the larger, tube-shaped fluorescent lights used by many businesses. A 15-watt CFL gives off the same amount of light as a regular 60-watt lightbulb, but it uses one-fourth of the electricity. The U.S. Environmental Protection Agency says that if we replace just one incandescent lightbulb in every U.S. household with a single CFL, we'd save enough power to light 3 million homes for a year! Handle them with care, clean them up properly if broken, and don't throw them away when they blow out — look online for CFL recycling locations.

LED stands for "light-emitting diode." *Di-* refers to "two." Inside each bulb are two kinds of crystals. When electricity flows into the bulb, its energy causes electrons to become excited in a **high-energy crystal.** The excited electrons jump off that crystal and into the **low-energy crystal.** The light is created by the energy that the electrons give off when they make this jump. LED lights use 85 percent less electricity than incandescent bulbs. Although the first kinds of LED lights showed up in the marketplace as holiday decorations, LEDs that can be used for regular lighting are quickly becoming more common and affordable.

LED LIGHTS USE 85 PERCENT LESS ELECTRICITY THAN INCANDESCENT BULBS.

PHANTOM POWER GHOST BUSTERS

When you get into bed and pull up the covers for the night, did you know that phantoms are haunting your home's power supply — sucking electricity from the grid as you dream? All of those warm little boxes attached to cell-phone chargers, computers, cordless phones, and other electronics use about 2 watts of power even when the devices are turned off. And all the appliances that have an "instant on" switch draw electricity 24/7, simply to make sure the switch is "live" when you turn it on. This means we're using energy while appliances are turned off, just so we don't have to wait a few seconds when we turn them on! This background energy drain is called *phantom power.*

In the United States, the phantom power we use to feed many of our electrical devices when they're turned off is now greater than the amount of power we use when they're actually switched on!

What can you do? In many European countries, there is a little switch on each electrical wall socket that can be turned off just before bedtime to cut the phantom power draw. You can do the same thing by plugging phantom-power devices into *surge strips* — those long narrow boxes with rows of outlets and a master switch that turns them off. "But," your parents or teachers might ask, "what about power for the computer that automatically 'backs up' my data at midnight?" For that situation you can get a Smart Strip, which has a few outlets that remain powered even when the others are switched off.

Like electro-vampires, transformer plugs suck energy even when electrical devices are switched off.

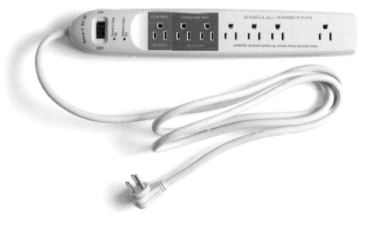

Energy-saving surge protectors, like the Smart Strip (above) and the Watt Stopper, take a bite out of phantom power energy drain.

POWER PLAY BOARD GAME

POWER PLAY IS ALL ABOUT USING AS LITTLE ELECTRICITY AS POSSIBLE. **WINNERS CAN FEEL THEIR POWER** — BY USING LESS ENERGY!

WHAT YOU WILL NEED

* � Template for game board (page 205)

* Air-dry clay, the kind that hardens when exposed to the air

* Fine-tipped colored markers

* Heavy-duty poster board that measures 22 × 28 inches (56 × 71 cm)

* Pencil with eraser

* Scissors

* Tube of scrapbook glue or a glue stick

* Pad of paper, for keeping score

* Pair of dice (can be borrowed from another game)

DO THE DEED

With each roll of the dice, each player moves his or her piece around the board, landing on places where they might waste energy or save energy. The biggest energy saver in the game — the one who has collected the fewest number of watts at the end — is the winner. In many places during the game, the score of the dice represents the number of watts of energy that is being either saved or wasted during that player's turn.

SCULPT YOUR OWN PLAYING PIECES

Using colored, air-dry modeling clay, sculpt the playing pieces that you want to use for the Power Play game — things that remind you of creating renewable energy or of ways to save energy. For example, you could sculpt a tiny windmill, bicycle, tree, piece of firewood, or electric car. Just remember that each piece will need to stand up on its own while it moves around the game board. Allow these pieces to dry until hard, then add details using the fine-tipped colored markers.

WHY FOSSIL FOOLS?

Fossil means "hopelessly out of date." This describes both fossil fuels (coal, oil and natural gas) and nuclear energy, which produces dangerous radioactive wastes that last millions of years. Fossil fuels hurt people and the planet through oil spills, strip mines, coalmines, and air pollution — including smog, greenhouse gases and acid rain. We can't create any more fossil fuels, and they're only found in certain places, so people often fight over them. Isn't it time to make our use of fossil fuels become *extinct?*

POWER PLAY!

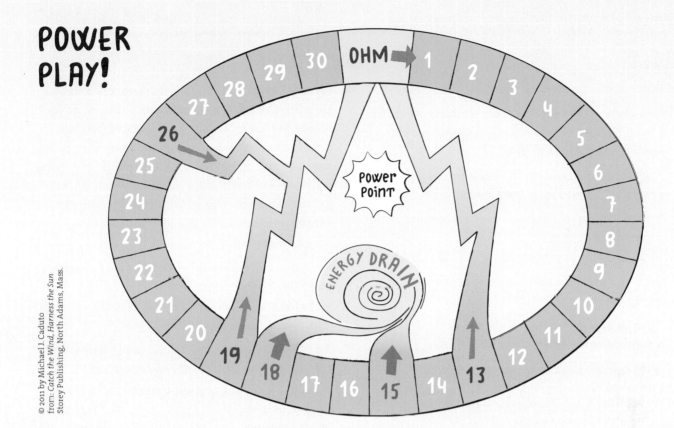

Your game board should look something like this.
Add your own colors and art.

PREPARING THE GAME BOARD

1 Draw a circular path on your poster board (see diagram above). Divide the path into 31 rectangular spaces. The largest space should be at the top of the circle. This space is called "Ohm." Add Power Point just below Ohm and above Energy Drain in the center of the board. You can draw images and pathways connecting spaces around the board that relate to what is written on page 207. Be creative!

2 Photocopy page 207. (If you don't have access to a photocopier, you can copy the actions onto your poster by hand.)

3 Using your scissors, cut out the actions for each space so that you have a total of 30 actions.

4 Arrange the actions in order, so that action 1 is to the right of Ohm and the other actions follow clockwise around the circle.

5 Glue each action (piece of paper) to the board, locating it in the appropriate space.

6 Now you're ready to play! Follow the rules on page 206 and roll your way to energy efficiency!

RULES

- Every player starts with 100 watts (points).
- One player is the scorekeeper. That person keeps a running tally of how many watts each player has at the end of each turn.
- Players should position their handmade game pieces on Ohm to start the game.
- Play moves sunwise (clockwise) around the game board.
- To start: Players take turns making one roll of the dice. The player who roles the lowest score plays first.
- When it's a player's turn, that player rolls the dice and moves forward that number of spaces.
- After moving their piece, players do whatever it says to do on each space they land on, adding or subtracting watts to their score as directed.

LOW-ENERGY ROLLS

- Power Play: A player who rolls 1s on both dice goes directly to Ohm and subtracts 20 watts from his or her score. (Although this is rolling doubles, it's the lowest — least energy — roll possible, so it earns a special bonus play.)
- A player who lands directly on the Ohm space on any given turn gets a free roll.

FOSSIL FOOL ROLLS

- When a player rolls doubles (any except two 1's), she adds the total number of watts shown on the dice to her score. Doubles are not Low-Energy Rolls because this game is about doing things in a new way and not repeating our bad energy habits. Doubles = a bad habit repeated. A player that rolls doubles not only adds the total number of the roll onto her wattage score but also moves the game piece and rolls again.
- If a player rolls doubles twice in a row, he adds twice the total of watts shown on the dice to his score the second time, then makes that move and rolls again.
- If a player rolls doubles three times in a row, she goes directly to the Energy Drain.
- Players remain in the Energy Drain until they roll a 1 or 2 on at least one of the dice. Until that time, players in the Energy Drain continue to roll and for each turn add the number of watts on the dice to their score. When a roll frees a player from the Energy Drain, that player places the playing piece back at Ohm, then moves that piece by the number shown on the dice.

(NOTE: *This does not necessarily end his play. He may have rolled two 1s or two 2s to get out of the Energy Drain, in which case he would go to Ohm, move that number of spaces, and roll again.*)

WINNING THE GAME

The first player who loses all of her watts wins the game and gets to move her piece to the Power Point.

   If you have to set a time limit at the beginning of the game, then the winner is whoever has the lowest number of watts when the designated time arrives. This means the winner is the player who has used the least amount of energy by the end of the game.

GAME BOARD SPECIAL SPACES

Ohm *(the space where the game begins)*

Energy Drain *(place where players go when they roll doubles three times in a row)*

Power Point *(winning energy-saver's place of honor)*

GAME BOARD ACTIONS FOR SPACES LANDED UPON

1 Electricity from your solar panels flowed into the grid. Subtract 5 watts.

2 You've been an energy hog all day. Add 5 watts.

3 You installed a smart meter so you can add power into the power pool. Subtract 15 watts.

4 You opened the refrigerator six times during breakfast. Add 6 watts.

5 You installed a home-sized windmill. Subtract 12 watts.

6 You now heat water with the Sun. Subtract 6 watts.

7 You have ten devices with instant-on switches that are always plugged in. Add 6 watts.

8 You drained your cell-phone battery talking for 2 hours straight and can't even recall what was said. Add 7 watts.

9 You rode your bicycle instead of riding in the car. Subtract 4 watts.

10 You used a dishwasher instead of doing dishes by hand. Add 4 watts.

11 You drove to pick up take-out food when you could have made a nice meal at home. Add 4 watts.

12 You switched to a windup alarm clock. Subtract 1 watt.

13 You convinced a friend to join you in setting up a *Catch the Wind, Harness the Sun* energy-saving group. Go directly to Ohm and subtract 20 watts.

14 You turned down your thermostat to 65°F (18°C) in the winter. Subtract 9 watts.

15 You spent a whole day playing computer games. Go directly to the Energy Drain and add 20 watts.

16 You replaced one incandescent lightbulb with a compact fluorescent. Subtract 3 watts.

17 You now turn off every light as you leave a room. Subtract 6 watts.

18 You got a ride to the store when you could have walked or biked. Go directly to the Energy Drain and add 20 watts.

19 You set up your Personal Solar Panel and are ready to go . . . directly to Ohm. Subtract 20 watts.

20 You carpooled with a friend's family to the soccer game. Subtract 4 watts.

21 You dried your clothes in a clothes dryer instead of on a clothesline. Add 10 watts.

22 You played outside all day. Subtract 12 watts.

23 You turned off the water while brushing your teeth. Subtract 2 watts.

24 You said "plastic" at the grocery counter instead of taking your own cloth shopping bag. Add 2 watts.

25 You're going to shut off your computer for 1 hour each day and do something fun outside. Subtract 8 watts.

26 You installed solar panels to power your whole house. Circle the board twice and then advance directly to Ohm. Subtract 40 watts!

27 You keep leaving on lights when you leave a room. Add 10 watts.

28 You walked to the store instead of driving. Subtract 4 watts.

29 You plugged several appliances into a surge strip to cut the phantom power use at night. Subtract 7 watts.

30 You opened a curtain to let in the sunlight for reading. Subtract 3 watts.

THE TREE OF WISDOM

(A Yoruba tale from Nigeria)

Tortoise stood beneath a Tree and thought about wisdom. He knew that gold held great value in the eyes of many. "But wisdom," he thought, "is worth more than anything else in the world."

Taking up a hollow calabash, a large bottle gourd, he tied it around his neck and went in search of wisdom. When passersby dropped morsels of wisdom during their conversations along the road, he picked them up and put them into his gourd. When the wisdom contained in the seeds of grain or in the nuts of trees fell to the ground or when a fluffy seed blew in on the breeze, Tortoise was there to snatch it up. If a bird's wisdom fluttered down from the sky in one of its feathers, Tortoise grabbed it with his beak and put it into the gourd. After many days of gathering and gleaning wisdom, the gourd was full.

As he gazed into his gourd, Tortoise thought, "Surely I am now the wisest of all. No one has ever gathered so much wisdom. This must be all there is in the world."

But now Tortoise was worried that someone might find his wisdom and steal it.

"I will put it up into this ancient baobab tree," he thought, looking at its wide spread of branches. "No one will ever find it there."

Tortoise hung the gourd full of wisdom around his neck and tried to climb the tree, but the gourd hung down by his belly and got in the way. He tried hanging it from one front leg and then the other front leg, but each time the weight of the gourd pulled him down and he fell off the tree. He tried tying it to his puny tail, but the rope kept slipping off. Then he tried holding it in his mouth, but he was so used to saying his thoughts out loud that he found he couldn't think clearly when his mouth was full.

Finally, he heard a small voice coming from the bush. "Hello, Tortoise."

"Where are you?" asked Tortoise, looking around.

"I'm down here."

"Oh, it's you, Snail," said Tortoise.

"That's no way to carry a gourd up a tree," said Snail.

"Well, then . . . how would you do it?" asked Tortoise curtly.

"Granted, I do not possess the wealth of wisdom that you do," admitted Snail, "but you might want to try tying the gourd onto the middle of your back, so the weight will be even and your limbs free to climb up the bark."

Tortoise stared at Snail and said nothing for a very long time. "Well," he snipped, "thank you for the words of wisdom."

Snail helped Tortoise to tie the gourd onto his back and watched as Tortoise made his way slowly up the tree and out onto one of its upper branches.

When Tortoise had caught his breath, he felt satisfied at holding all the wisdom in the world inside his gourd, which was now safely hidden in the tree. But then another thought began to eat at him.

"If I hold all the wisdom in the world inside this gourd," he thought, "then why is it that I needed advice from Snail to get the gourd up into this tree?"

At that moment, Tortoise realized that no matter how much wisdom he gathered, there would always be more to learn. So he untied the gourd from his back, dropped it from up in the tree, and watched as it smashed on the ground, planting some of its wisdom in the soil and scattering the rest to the winds.

It's not surprising that a tortoise, a gourd, and a baobab tree are found in a story about wisdom. Turtles and tortoises are thought to be wise, perhaps because they live long and never seem to rush into anything. Many native cultures believe that plants store wisdom in their seeds, and hollowed-out gourds are used as seed containers.

If age brings wisdom, then a baobab tree must also be very wise. It can live for more than 2,000 years, can grow taller than 80 feet (24 m), and can measure over 90 feet (27 m) around its gigantic trunk. Many traditional peoples who live in the grasslands of Africa still meet under the spreading branches of this "Tree of Life" when they want to tell stories, to teach, or to learn something important.

A book is not a baobab tree, but it is a powerful tool for sharing knowledge and wisdom. Ideas from a book can be gathered and stored in your mind, just as Tortoise filled up his gourd. The **knowledge** found in *Catch the Wind, Harness the Sun* gives you the facts and skills you need in order to know *how* to begin living in a way that is powered by renewable energy.

Wisdom, however, tells you *why* it is important to take care of the planet. And as Tortoise discovered, there is always more to learn. Now you are ready to scatter the seeds of wisdom to the wind and help to grow a better world — one that is powered by energy that can sustain the generations to come.

EPILOGUE

"UNLESS SOMEONE LIKE YOU CARES A WHOLE AWFUL LOT, NOTHING IS GOING TO GET BETTER, IT'S NOT."

— The Once-ler, in *The Lorax* by Dr. Seuss

Even though you've now come to the end of *Catch the Wind, Harness the Sun*, your journey to capture renewable energy and conserve power is just beginning. Life is one colossal Power Play game with billions of players. Every time someone harnesses renewable energy or saves energy by living wisely, all of humankind and every part of the natural world move closer to winning.

But let's not leave it up to a roll of the dice. It's time to set some goals and plan for a bright future that shines from kids who care about Planet Earth. Parents may teach the wisdom of elders to the next generation, but kids are able to see the things around them with new eyes. Young people are at the leading edge of the positive changes that are happening to make the world a better place.

Because youths make up more than 25 percent of the world's 6.8 billion people, you have a vast global voice that can speak for our Earth. The power of kids is in changing habits and helping environmental leaders to take us into a new day, when our lives are powered by the unlimited forces of nature.

Green Giant Adeline Tiffanie Suwana (third from right) and members of Sahabat Alam, "Friends of Nature," pose in front of the Electric Generator Water Reel they built to capture the power of a waterfall. Their project introduced electricity to the Indonesian village of Kampung Cilulumpang in West Java.

APPENDIX

ACTIVITY EXTRA

MINI-WINDMILL POWER

SPECIAL WINDMILL DESIGN FOR AREAS WITH LIGHT WIND

Here is a version of the rotor and tail assembly for the Mini-Windmill described on page 160 that can be used in places where the wind speed is slow much of the time. This design will keep the Mini-Windmill blades spinning and facing into light winds.

NOTE: The parts listed with an asterisk (*) on pages 211 and 212 come with the Mini-Windmill Kit recommended for the Mini-Windmill Power activity on page 161 (see Resources for kit ordering information). You will need to obtain other parts and tools separately.

MATERIALS FOR MAKING THE LONGER WINDMILL TAIL AND TAIL FIN

* Tape measure
* One 30-inch- (76 cm) long piece of wooden clapboard
* Pencil
* Straightedge
* Ruler
* Safety goggles
* Handsaw
* 1 piece of medium-grit (#80) sandpaper
* 2 galvanized Phillips-head screws measuring ½ inch (1.25 cm) long (for attaching the tail fin)
* Phillips-head screwdriver

* 1 T-shaped metal bracket, on which to mount the motor and tail fin (about ¾ inch [2 cm] wide × 13 inches [33 cm] long)*
* Electric drill and ¼-inch (6 mm) drill bit
* 2 machine bolts measuring 1.5 inches (4 cm) long × ¼-inch (6 mm) in diameter (for attaching the tail to the T-shaped metal bracket)*
* 2 flat ("fender") washers for the ¼-inch- (6 mm) diameter machine bolts*
* 2 matching ¼-inch (6 mm) nuts for the machine bolts*
* 2 small adjustable wrenches

MATERIALS FOR MAKING THE SIX-BLADED WINDMILL ROTOR

* **Three 17-inch- (43 cm) long PVC windmill blades with holes drilled for bolting to the plastic disk** (see Resources for obtaining three blades in addition to the three that come in the standard Mini-Windmill kit)

* **One 5-inch- (13 cm) diameter, round plastic disk made of ³⁄₁₆-inch (0.5 cm) ABS plastic with holes drilled for attaching windmill blades*** (see Resources for obtaining the disk that comes in the standard Mini-Windmill kit)

* **Pencil or pen**

* **Ruler**

* **Electric drill and ¼-inch (6 mm) drill bit**

* **6 machine bolts measuring 1 inch (2.5 cm) long × ¼-inch (6 mm) in diameter**

* **6 flat ("fender") washers for the ¼-inch- (6 mm) diameter machine bolts**

* **6 matching ¼-inch (6 mm) nuts for the machine bolts**

* **2 small adjustable wrenches**

BUYING OR MAKING THE BLADES

USA Wind Generators (see page 216) is a source for the three additional 17-inch- (43 cm) long PVC windmill blades listed above. Specify that you want to order the blades that are normally shipped with the 50-watt, mini–wind turbine.

Alternatively, you can make your own turbine blades by using 4-inch- (10 cm) diameter, narrow-gauge (⅛-inch- [3 mm] thick) PVC pipe. Just lay an existing turbine blade down onto the outside of the *flared* end of the PVC pipe, then trace around it. Cut along that line with a narrow-bladed handsaw or a saber saw, then round off the edges with a file and sand them smooth with medium-grit sandpaper. Drill two, ¼-inch (6 mm) holes on the wider end, in exactly the same location that they are found in the turbine blades that came with your Mini-Windmill kit.

! SAFETY FIRST !

Be sure to have an adult supervise and help you when using the handsaw and electric drill. Always protect your eyes with safety goggles when cutting or drilling.

DO THE DEED

Use these materials and directions to modify the design given in the Mini-Windmill Power activity. You will be adding three additional 17-inch- (43 cm) long PVC windmill blades to the ABS plastic disk (for six blades total) plus a longer tail to the T-shaped metal bracket. (See photo on page 211.)

MAKING THE LONGER WINDMILL TAIL AND TAIL FIN

1 Measure 6 inches (15 cm) in from one end of the clapboard and mark this location with the pencil. Using the straightedge or ruler as a guide, draw a straight line from top to bottom across the clapboard and at a 90 degree angle (right angle) to the edge.

2 Use the handsaw to cut off this 6-inch piece of clapboard. Set aside this piece to use later for making the tail fin.

3 Cut the long piece of clapboard so that it measures 3 inches (8 cm) wide along its entire length. Use the ruler and pencil to make several marks that are 3 inches in from the thick edge.

4 Use the straightedge and the pencil to connect these marks. This creates a line along the length of the clapboard that is 3 inches in from the thick edge.

5 Steady the clapboard along the edge of a workbench or worktable and carefully cut along this line using the handsaw. This 3-inch-wide strip of clapboard will be the tail for your light-wind Mini-Windmill.

6 Take the 6-inch (15 cm) piece you cut off the clapboard in Step 2. Using the tape measure and pencil, make two marks: one mark in the middle of the long, thin edge and one mark in the middle of the side edge. Now draw a diagonal line that joins these two marks across that corner.

7 Cut along this line with the handsaw to make the tail fin.

8 Use the sandpaper to smooth off all rough edges on the tail and the tail fin.

9 Lay the tail on a flat surface. Now place the tail fin on top so that it overlaps the tail by about 3 inches (8 cm). Line up the bottom of the tail fin with the bottom of the tail, so that the cut-off corner is on top and facing the windmill blades.

10 Using the Phillips-head screwdriver and the two galvanized Phillips-head screws, attach the tail fin to the tail.

11 Line up the bottom edge of the other (thin) end of the tail with the lower edge of the T-shaped metal bracket on which the windmill rotor is mounted. Hold the tail so that it overlaps the two holes in the metal.

12 While holding the tail and metal bracket so that they're lined up together, stick a pencil through the holes in the metal bracket and make marks where you will need to drill the two bolt holes in the clapboard.

13 Drill the two ¼-inch (6 mm) holes in the tail.

14 Slip the two 1.5-inch- (4 cm) long × ¼-inch (6 mm) bolts through the holes in the T-shaped metal bracket, then slide the holes in the end of the tail down over the ends of the bolts.

15 Slip a metal washer over the end of each bolt, then screw on the nuts by hand. Use the two adjustable wrenches to snug the nuts down onto the bolts.

MAKING THE SIX-BLADED WINDMILL ROTOR

1 Obtain three additional 17-inch- (43 cm) long PVC windmill blades like the three blades you attached while putting together your Mini-Windmill. (See Resources to find out how you can obtain these blades.)

2 Use a pencil or pen and ruler to mark two holes that are in between each of the three existing pairs of bolt holes in the round plastic disk. Make sure the new holes are placed exactly in between each set of existing holes, and the same distance in from the edge of the disk. Use the two holes on the wide end of one of the original turbine blades as a guide for locating these new holes on the plastic disk.

3 Carefully drill all six of the new bolt holes using the ¼-inch (6 mm) drill bit.

4 Use the six 1-inch (2.5 cm) machine bolts to attach the three new windmill blades to the round plastic hub (two bolts for each blade). Place the flat surface on the wide end of each blade up against the round hub, so the inside of the curve will face the wind. Slip the bolts through from the front side of the blades and then through the round plastic hub. Attach a flat washer and nut onto the threaded end of each bolt, then use the adjustable wrenches to tighten firmly but not too tight.

5 Reassemble the Mini-Windmill Power station, starting with step 9 on page 167.

RESOURCES

GREEN GIANT WEBSITES

- **Adeline Tiffanie Suwana**
  http://sahabat-alam.com/en
- **Cameron Oliver**
  www.cameronscamelcampaign.com
- **Colin Carlson**
  http://webpages.charter.net/cool_coventry_club/home.htm
- **Idle Free Girls and Nathan Moos**
  www.climatechangeconnection.org
  Website of Climate Change Connection, where you can obtain Idle Free Zone Signs.
- **Kevin Huo**
  http://birdsoverthebay.blogspot.com
- **Michelle Marcus**
  http://greenandcleanearth.wordpress.com
- **Otana Jakpor**
  http://witheverybreath.org

PARTS 1 & 2
HEATING UP AND CHILLING OUT (GLOBAL CLIMATE CHANGE)

ACTIVITY SUPPLY SOURCES

World Map for Helping Countries on the Hot Seat

- **MapCenter.com**
  888-568-6277
  http://mapcenter.com
  Click on World Maps
- **Maps of World**
  408-326-9371
  www.mapsofworld.com
- **National Geographic**
  800-437-5521
  http://maps.nationalgeographic.com/maps

ORGANIZATIONS

- **The Alliance for Climate Protection**
  www.climateprotect.org
- **Climate Action Network (CAN) International**
  202-621-6309
  www.climatenetwork.org

- **The Climate Project**
  615-327-7577
  www.theclimateprojectus.org
- **Environmental Defense Fund**
  800-684-3322
  www.edf.org

SOURCES THAT EXPLAIN GLOBAL CLIMATE CHANGE

- **Energy Kids**
  U.S. Energy Information Administration
  202-586-8800
  http://tonto.eia.doe.gov/kids/?featureclicked=5&
- **Global Greenhouse Gases**
  U.S. Energy Information Administration
  http://tonto.eia.doe.gov/energyexplained/index.cfm?page=environment_where_ghg_come_from
- **Global Warming Question and Answer Web Site**
  National Oceanic and Atmospheric Administration/ National Environmental Satellite, Data, and Information Service (NESDIS)
  www.ncdc.noaa.gov/oa/climate/globalwarming.html#q1
- **Greenhouse Gases and Society**
  University of Michigan
  www.umich.edu/~gs265/society/greenhouse.htm
- **Tiki the Penguin — oneclimate.net**
  http://tiki.oneworld.net/global_warming/climate_home.html

PART 3
HARNESS THE SUN (SOLAR POWER)

ACTIVITY SUPPLY SOURCES

Solar Cooker Plans

- **Solar Cooking Archive**
  www.solarcooking.org/plans
- **Bernard Solar Panel Cooker**
  http://solarcooking.org/plans/spc.htm

Personal Solar Power Supplies

- **Sundance Solar Products, Inc.**
  603-225-2020
  http://store.sundancesolar.com/do-it-yourself-solar-kits.html
  Source for a reasonably-priced kit that contains all the components needed to make your Personal Solar Power Station. Order the "10-Watt Economy Do it Yourself Kit."

RESOURCES

12-Volt Appliances

- **Direct Depot**
  888-797-4321
  www.directdepot.net
- **Boat & RV Accessories**
  937-231-8822
  www.boatandrvaccessories.com

FURTHER INFORMATION

Structure of Atoms

- **Atomic Structure**
  http://web.jjay.cuny.edu/~acarpi/NSC/3-atoms.htm
- **Rader's Chem4Kids**
  www.chem4kids.com/files/atom_structure.html

Biomass Energy

- **CVPS Cow Power**
  Central Vermont Public Service
  800-649-2877
  www.cvps.com/cowpower/How%20It%20Works.html

Monarch Butterfly Migration

- **Journey North**
  www.learner.org/jnorth/tm/monarch/HeightFallFlight.html
- **Monarch Watch Monarch Waystation Program**
  University of Kansas
  888-824-4464
  www.monarchwatch.org/waystations

NASA Sun & Earth Background

- **National Aeronautics and Space Administration**
  http://stargazers.gsfc.nasa.gov/resources/sun_earth_background.htm

Neon Lights and Other Colored Gases

- **Luminous Artworks**
  www.luminousartworks.com/index.html
  Click on "How Neon Works" and "What Makes the Colors" in the "Resources" menu.

Solar Energy for Students and Educators

- **Solar Energy International**
  970-963-8855
  www.solarenergy.org/resources/kids.html
  Solar energy information for students and educators.

Traditional Oil Lamps

- **Absolute Astronomy**
  www.absoluteastronomy.com/topics/Oil_lamp

PART 4
CATCH THE WIND (WIND POWER)

ACTIVITY SUPPLY SOURCES

Idle Free Signs

- **EMEDCO (See also: Climate Change Connection)**
  866-222-4743
  www.emedco.com/endecasearch/result/query/?Ntt=idle&x=0&y=0

Mini-Windmill Power Station Kit

- **USA Wind Generators**
  505-717-7162
  www.usawindgen.com
  Order the 50 Watt Mini Wind Turbine. You can also find extra blades for use with the special windmill design for areas with light wind.

ORGANIZATIONS

- **Climate Change Connection**
  204-943-4836
  www.climatechangeconnection.org/
  Information on climate change and source of "Idle Free Zone" signs.
- **Idle Free Ontario**
  www.idlefreeontario.ca

FURTHER INFORMATION

Issues to Consider with Wind Power

- **Spirituality & Health**
  www.spiritualityhealth.com/spirit/archives/how-make-your-own-wind-power
  Issues to consider when building a larger wind turbine on your property.

Maps of Wind Energy

- **Environment Canada**
  www.windatlas.ca/en/maps.php
  This agency has posted the Canadian Wind Energy Atlas. Click on the map location near where you live, then add the postal code for your location.
- **U.S. Department of Energy**
  www.windpoweringamerica.gov/wind_maps.asp
  Maps showing where wind speed is good for generating power. Click on your state map, then click on the place where you live to enlarge.

Not-So-Mini Windmill Power

⦿ **Vela Creations**
Instructables: Chispito Wind Generator
www.velacreations.com/chispito.html
Step-by-step instructions and issues to consider for making a larger homemade windmill.

Poul la Cour (Wind Energy Pioneer)

⦿ **Danish Wind Energy Association**
www.talentfactory.dk/en/pictures/lacour.htm
The association's guided tours have great information about wind energy and inventor Poul la Cour.

⦿ **Suite101.com**
www.suite101.com/content/poul-la-cour--danish-inventor-teacher-and-windmill-pioneer-a270767
Lots of information about this educator and pioneer.

Sculpture-Like Swedish Energy Ball

⦿ **Tree Hugger (Discovery Communications)**
www.treehugger.com/files/2008/09/swedish-energy-ball-spherical-silent-home-wind-turbine.php

Toy Electric Car Powered by Wind Turbine

⦿ **Tree Hugger (Discovery Communications)**
www.treehugger.com/files/2007/08/wind_turbine_to_1.php

Vertical Small Wind Power Towers

⦿ **Quiet Revolution**
www.quietrevolution.co.uk

PART 5
CRANK UP THE POWER (ELECTROMAGNETIC ENERGY)

ACTIVITY SUPPLY SOURCES

Magnetism and Magnet Kits
In addition to the following online sources, many toy stores and hobby shops carry basic, inexpensive science magnet kits that contain several magnets, iron filings, and materials for a variety of electromagnetic experiments.

⦿ **Discover This: Educational Science Kits & Toys**
866-438-8697
www.discoverthis.com/magnets-kits.html

⦿ **Edmunds Scientifics (Science With Magnets Kit)**
800-728-6999
http://scientificsonline.com/product.asp_Q_pn_E_3081443

⦿ **PhysLink.com: Science eStore**
www.physlink.com/eStore/cart/Magnets.cfm

Pedal Power Station: Bicycle Stand
Google "bicycle trainer fitness stands" for Web sites, sources, and information.

Pedal Power Station: 12-volt DC Generator (Geared Motor) and Metal Arbor

⦿ **USA Wind Generators**
505-717-7162
www.usawindgen.com
This is the same generator used on the Mini-Windmill Power station. Order the same geared generator that comes with the 50 Watt Mini Wind Turbine, including the 1-inch metal arbor that mounts on the generator shaft.

Pedal Power Station: Bicycle Generator
Use as a mounting bracket for the 12-volt generator.

⦿ **BikeWorld USA**
518-831-1751
www.bikeworldusa.com/product_info.php/products_id/394?osCsid=9a3e5068334835ffd2e9ec60e527c1c8

Pedal Power Station: 12-Volt DC Gear Motors for Use as Generators (Alternatives)

⦿ **CMACMA Technologies**
406-842-5339
www.cmacma.com
Specify part numbers AST-0341-5 and AST-9941-5. The 12-volt generator must fit onto the mount described in the Pedal Power station and generate 12-volts of power at about 200-300 hundred rpm's.

FURTHER INFORMATION

Electricity History: Origins and Inventions

⦿ **The Electricity Forum**
www.electricityforum.com/electricity-history.html.

Electric Motors and Generators: How They Work

⦿ **The Electricity Forum — Polycast International**
www.wvic.com/how-gen-works.htm

⦿ **University of New South Wales, School of Physics, Sydney, Australia**
www.animations.physics.unsw.edu.au/jw/electricmotors.html

RESOURCES

Ginger Ninjas

904-608-0139

http://gingerninjas.com/

Website for rock band that travels by bicycle and electrifies their performances with pedal power.

Hydrogen Fuel Cells

- ⊘ **howstuffworks (Discovery Co.)**

  http://auto.howstuffworks.com/fuel-efficiency/alternative-fuels/fuel-cell.htm

  Information and a video explaining how hydrogen fuel cells work and how they can be used to provide renewable energy.

Large-Scale Pedal Power Station Plans

- ⊘ **Pedal Power Bike Generators**

  http://scienceshareware.com/bicycle-generator-faq.htm#choosing-ratings

Play Pumps in Africa

- ⊘ **Roundabout Water Solutions**

  www.playpumps.co.za

  Information on how PlayPumps in Africa work, with photos and a video showing children using PlayPumps.

Static Electricity and Experiments

- ⊘ **Science Made Simple**

  www.sciencemadesimple.com/static.html

MORE WEBSITES FOR KIDS

- ⊘ **The Big Blue Bus (Aquatic Life)**

  Fisheries and Oceans, Canada

  www.dfo-mpo.gc.ca/canwaters-eauxcan/bbb-lgb/

- ⊘ **Eco Friendly Kids (UK)**

  http://ecofriendlykids.co.uk

- ⊘ **EcoKids: Earth Day Canada**

  www.ecokids.ca/pub/index.cfm

- ⊘ **Energy Kids' Page**

  U.S. Energy Information Administration

  http://tonto.eia.doe.gov/kids

- ⊘ **Environment Canada: Kids & Youth**

  www.ec.gc.ca/education/defaultasp?lang=En&n=51ccecc2-1

- ⊘ **Oracle Think Quest**

  Oracle Education Foundation

  www.thinkquest.org/en

  Click the Library tab, then Science & Technology for a list of student websites around the world.

CURRICULUM CONNECTIONS

- ⊘ **GreenLearning Canada**

  613-256-1487

  www.greenlearning.ca

- ⊘ **NASA Science Website for Teachers & Parents**

  202-358-0001

  http://search.nasa.gov/search/edFilterSearch.jsp?empty=true

- ⊘ **Natural Resources Canada: Climate Change Teacher Resources**

  613-995-0947

  http://adaptation.nrcan.gc.ca/posters/curriculum/index_e.php

- ⊘ **Northeast Sustainable Energy Association's free Curricular Units (K–12)**

  413-774-6051

  www.nesea.org/k-12/curricularunits

- ⊘ **The Pembina Foundation: Energy Lessons, Activities & Curriculum Links**

  780-542-2865

  www.pembinafoundation.org

- ⊘ **U.S. Department of Energy: K-12 Lesson Plans & Activities**

  877-337-3463

  www1.eere.energy.gov/education/lessonplans

HELPING COUNTRIES ON THE HOT SEAT

SOME ANIMALS THREATENED & ENDANGERED BY GLOBAL CLIMATE CHANGE
(brief list by continent)

Africa
African Lion (*Panthera leo*)
African Penguin (*Spheniscus demersus*)
Chimpanzee (*Pan troglodytes*)
Congo Serpent-eagle (*Dryotriorchis spectabilis*)
African Elephant (*Loxodonta africana*)
Madagascar Pochard (*Aythya innotata*)
Ring-tailed Lemur (*Lemur catta*)
Violet-tailed Sunbird (*Anthreptes aurantium*)

Antarctica
Blue Whale (*Balaenoptera musculus*)
Emperor Penguin (*Aptenodytes forsteri*)
King Penguin (*Aptenodytes patagonicus*)
Macaroni Penguin (*Eudyptes chrysolophus*)
Northern Rockhopper Penguin (*Eudyptes moseleyi*)
Sea Butterfly (*Clione antarctica*)
Southern Right Whale (*Eubalaena australis*)

Asia
Arctic Fox (*Alopex lagopus* or *Vulpes lagopus*)
Beluga Whale (*Delphinapterus leucas*)
Bengal Tiger (*Panthera tigris tigris*)
Asian Elephant (*Elephas maximus*)
Giant Panda (*Ailuropoda melanoleuca*)
Polar Bear (*Ursus maritimus*)
Snowy Owl (*Bubo scandiacus*)
Susu, or Ganges River Dolphin (*Platanista gangetica gangetica*)

Australia and Oceania
Black Flying Fox (*Pteropus alecto*)
Flowerpot Coral (*Alveopora allingi*)
'I'iwi or Hawaiian Honeycreeper (*Vestiaria coccinea*)
Koala (*Phascolarctos cinereus*)
Laysan Albatross (*Phoebastria immutabilis*)
Mountain Pygmy-possum (*Burramys parvus*)
Southern Rockhopper Penguin (*Eudyptes chrysocome*)

Europe
Harp Seal (*Phoca groenlandica*)
Ivory Gull (*Pagophila eburnea*)
Narwhal (*Monodon monoceros*)
Red-breasted Goose (*Branta ruficollis*)
Small Tortoiseshell Butterfly (*Aglais urticae*)
Spoon-billed Sandpiper (*Eurynorhynchus pygmeus*)
Steller's Eider (*Polysticta stelleri*)
Yellow-billed Loon (*Gavia adamsii*)

North America
Caribou (*Rangifer tarandus*)
False Killer Whale (*Pseudorca crassidens*)
Gray Whale (*Eschrichtius robustus*)
Musk Ox (*Ovibos moschatus*)
North Atlantic Right Whale (*Eubalaena glacialis*)
North Pacific Right Whale (*Eubalaena japonica*)
Pacific Walrus (*Odobenus rosmarus divergens*)
Polar Bear (*Ursus maritimus*)
Puget Sound Killer Whale (*Orcinus orca*)
Resplendent Quetzal (*Pharomachrus mocinno*)
White-tailed Ptarmigan (*Lagopus leucura*)

South America
Boto or Amazon River Dolphin (*Inia geoffrensis*)
Colombian Woolly Monkey (*Lagothrix lugens*)
Galapagos Penguin (*Spheniscus mendiculus*)
Harlequin Poison Frog (*Dendrobates histrionicus*)
Humboldt Penguin (*Spheniscus humboldti*)
Lehmann's Poison Frog (*Dendrobates lehmanni*)
Red Howler Monkey (*Alouatta seniculus*)

Worldwide
Fin Whale (*Balaenoptera physalus*)
Flatback Sea Turtle (*Natator depressus*)
Green Sea Turtle (*Chelonia mydas*)
Hawksbill Sea Turtle (*Eretmochelys imbricata*)
Kemp's Ridley Sea Turtle (*Lepidochelys kempii*)
Leatherback Sea Turtle (*Dermochelys coriacea*)
Loggerhead Sea Turtle (*Caretta caretta*)
Olive Ridley Sea Turtle (*Lepidochelys olivacea*)
Sperm Whale (*Physeter macrocephalus*)

ACKNOWLEDGMENTS

More than any other book I've written, *Catch the Wind, Harness the Sun* is a true collaboration of hearts and minds. The vision and commitment of many people at Storey Publishing helped to bring this book to life. Publisher Pam Art saw the book's potential from the start, as did Acquiring Editor Deborah Burns, who also shepherded the manuscript through its early, formative stages. Rebekah L. Boyd-Owens, Editor, contributed a tremendous amount of creative energy and ideas that helped to sculpt the manuscript into its final form. Editor Sarah Guare and Art Director Jessica Armstrong envisioned and shaped the raw text and images into this wonderful publication.

Experts who reviewed the manuscript for accuracy include Cynthia Grippaldi, education coordinator at the Center for Ecological Technology (CET) in Pittsfield, Massachusetts; Susan Reyes, Science Educator, Northeast Sustainable Energy Association (NESEA); Benjamin P. Luce, Ph.D., Assistant Professor of Physics and Sustainability Studies, Lyndon State College; and my wife, Marie Levesque Caduto, watershed planner for the Vermont Agency of Natural Resources, who has more than 20 years of experience in the field of environmental education. David Bonta — founder and owner/developer of the USA Solar Store licensing program — also reviewed the manuscript for accuracy and kindly offered to write a Foreword.

It took many eyes to read the text and field-test activities for accuracy. I'm grateful for help from the following teachers: Cathy Carrington, of Memorial Middle School in Middlefield, Connecticut; Patty Collins, of Reading Elementary School in Reading, Vermont; and Frank Kelley, of the Chester-Andover Elementary School in Chester, Vermont. Dr. Eugene Bernal, optometrist, of White River Junction, Vermont, provided guidance on eye care and safety for the activity Writing with Sunlight.

Two experts who helped tremendously by answering many of my questions on the designs for solar- and wind-power stations are Ed Bender, president of Sundance Solar Products, Inc., in Warner, New Hampshire, and Don Stutts, owner and founder of USA WInd Generators in Weed, New Mexico.

Except for the photographs of the Green Kids and a few others, the photography in *Catch the Wind, Harness the Sun* was framed by the discerning eye of Gregory Nesbit (Greg Nesbit Photography), and then both honed and edited by the expert vision of Storey Publishing's photo editor, Mars Vilaubi. Abigail Mnookin, science teacher at the Green Mountain Union High School in Chester, Vermont, kindly granted permission for use of the photograph of the wind farm on page 155.

Several people and organizations were critical in helping me to find and correspond with the Green Giants: Beryl Kay, president of Action For Nature; Reid Bodley, communications coordinator of Earth Day Canada; Lee Roy, EcoKids program coordinator of Earth Day Canada (EcoKids Challenge winners); Maia Green, founder, FUN Society and program director, FUN Camps; and Kari Kinley, who assists the Idle Free Girls in Stonewall, Manitoba.

I am especially grateful to the parents of all Green Giants and the Green Giants themselves.

Photographing the activities called for tremendous patience and good humor from all of the children and adults who appear in the many how-to images in *Catch the Wind, Harness the Sun*. Many thanks to the Chester-Andover Elementary School in Chester, Vermont, along with teacher Frank Kelley and members of his fifth-grade class: Brennan Adams, Ben Cutler, Jonathan Dion, Jared Jackson, Ian Kehoe, Sierra Kemp, Sean Kenney, Jesse R. Kendall, Aili Reitmeyer Lankone, Lori Martinez, Skye H. Tucker McCartney, Matthew Mosher, Cameron Peterson, Michael Randzio, Kenny Skinner, Alexandria M. Steele, Ashley Thomas, Molly Verespy, Skylar White, and Emily Williams. Parent helpers Domenica Pero Coger, Kelley Kehoe, Brant Nelson, Rebecca Salem, Michele Turner, and Mars Vilaubi donated their time and generously shared the enthusiasm and energy of their kids, including Aedan and Gwen Coger, Emma and Thalia Nelson, Jonah Salem, Rosalie Turner, and Xavier Vilaubi.

Heath Elementary School and the Pelham Lake Park Department in Rowe, Massachusetts gave us permission to photograph on their premises. Adult helpers included Laura Huff, Julie Seaver, and Park Ranger Sean Loomis. Many students were photographed while conducting activities: Alouette Batteau; Eleanora and Nathaniel Boyd-Owens; Sovahn Crawford; Julian and Oliver Diamond; Corinne and Charlotte Freeman; Kesheal Henderson; and Gabe, Lilly, and Emilia Seaver.

Light on!

INDEX

Page references in *italics* indicate photos or illustrations.

PHOTOGRAPHY CREDITS

Cover and interior photography by © Greg Nesbit Photography, except for:
© Abigail Mnookin: 155 top; © Amy Walters/Dreamstime.com: 4 left, 44–45; © Ben Beltman/iStockphoto.com: 54; © Bob Thomas/iStockphoto.com: 73; Courtesy of Cameron Oliver: 74, 75; © Elena Moiseeva/iStockphoto.com: 104; © esemelwe/iStockphoto.com: 32; © Ginger Ninjas stock photo: 200; Courtesy of Home Energy AB: 157; © Kevin Huo: 16–17; © Michael J. Caduto: 6, 7, 115; Courtesy of the author, Michael J. Caduto: 34, 64, 65, 98, 118, 119, 134, 158, 190, 191, 210; © Monirul Alam/Drik/Majority World: 72; Courtesy of NASA: 79, 83; © POUL LA COUR FOUNDATION: 147; Courtesy of Roundabout Water Solutions SA, www.playpumps.co.za: 189; © Serhiy Zavalnyuk/iStockphoto.com: 41; © Szeno/Dreamstime.com: 68; © Thomas Tuchan/iStockphoto.com: 84; © Trout 55/iStockphoto.com: 5 left, 130–131; Courtesy of United States Air Force, photo by Senior Airman Joshua Strang: 86; © Varin-Visage/Photo Researchers, Inc.: 71; © Vhawaya/Dreamstime.com: 5 right, 172–173; © W. Wacker/Wikimedia Commons: 155 bottom; © Yuliyan Velchev/Dreamstime.com: 4 right, 80–81

OTHER STOREY TITLES YOU WILL ENJOY

Nature's Art Box, *by Laura C. Martin.*
Cool projects for crafty kids to make with natural materials.
224 pages. Paper. ISBN 978-1-58017-490-9.

The Nature Connection, *by Clare Walker Leslie.*
An interactive workbook packed with creative, year-round nature activities.
304 pages. Paper. ISBN 978-1-60342-531-5.

Raptor! *by Christyna M. Laubach, Rene Laubach, and Charles W.G. Smith.*
A kid's guide to the birds at the top of the food chain: eagles, falcons, hawks, kites, ospreys, owls, and vultures.
128 pages. Paper. ISBN 978-1-58017-445-9.

Recycled Crafts Box, *by Laura C. Martin.*
Forty great craft projects using materials straight from the recycling bin.
96 pages. Paper. ISBN 978-1-58017-522-7.

Sewing School, *by Amie Petronis Plumley and Andria Lisle.*
Twenty-one inspired hand-sewing projects that kids can do with minimal supervision.
144 pages. Paper with concealed wire-o and flaps. ISBN 978-1-60342-578-0.

Trash-to-Treasure Papermaking, *by Arnold E. Grummer.*
Dozens of fabulous techniques and projects to transform any paper at hand — from wrapping paper to junk mail — into beautiful handmade paper.
208 pages. Paper. ISBN 978-1-60342-547-6.

WoodsWalk, *by Henry W. Art and Michael W. Robbins.*
A lively and fact-filled book introducing kids to the wonders of the natural world.
128 pages. Paper. ISBN 978-1-58017-452-7.
Hardcover with jacket. ISBN 978-1-58017-477-0.

These and other books from Storey Publishing are available wherever quality books are sold or by calling 1-800-441-5700.
Visit us at *www.storey.com*.